Navigating Life
With God's Compass

Insights and Practical Guidance
From Every Book of the Bible

"Your word is a lamp to my feet and a light to my path."
Psalm 119:105

*"Break open Your words, let the light shine out,
let ordinary people see the meaning."*
Psalm 119:130 (The Message Bible)

Daniel C. Rhodes

Destiny Navigators

Navigating Life
With God's Compass
Copyright © 2012
Daniel C. Rhodes—Destiny Navigators, LLC
Printed in United States of America

All rights reserved. This book is protected by the copyright laws of the United States of America and may not be copied or reprinted for commercial gain or profit. All Scripture quotations are from the New American Standard Bible : 1995 update. LaHabra, CA: The Lockman Foundation. Any variation is noted in parenthesis.

ISBN-13: 978-1478174059
ISBN-10: 1478174056

Destiny Navigators, LLC
Decatur, GA

www.DestinyNavigators.org
DanCRhodes@DestinyNavigators.org

Dedication

Across the years I have had the privilege of ministering to thousands of wonderful people from all walks of life and levels of faith. In all these years, I've never met a Christian who didn't want to discover God's will and purpose for their life. With the help of the Lord, I have been honored to assist them as they navigate their lives with the wisdom of His Word. Without God's Written Word and the Power of His Holy Spirit, we would most certainly lose our way and never achieve God's intentions for our lives!

To those who hunger and thirst for righteousness and who desire to walk in God's Destiny for their lives, I dedicate this book.

Acknowledgments

I am greatly indebted to the vast array of Biblical reference materials, commentators, Christian authors and Bible teachers that have formed a sound theological grid of Biblical truth and Christian thought in my life. Without that solid foundation, this book could never have been written nor would it have properly represented the truth of Scripture.

Special thanks are given to Randee and Joel Black of Black Bear Design Group. Randee's exceptional skills in graphic design created the amazing cover for this book. And Joel's remarkable website technology provided a state of the art media for posting and promoting these teachings through Destiny Navigators website.

Deep appreciation and gratitude is given to our youngest daughter, Anna Lindsey, and her husband. Her skillful assistance in copy-editing this work for grammatical correctness and flow of thought is irreplaceable. I am especially honored for Anna to work on this project with me because she lives what I write, as does our oldest daughter, Jenny Querubin, and her husband.

Endorsements

There are books written about the Scriptures and then there are Scriptural books. This is one of those extraordinary works. The author navigates us through the historic texts and extracts wisdom and counsel. He allows the prophets to speak to us plainly with meaningful corrections and instructions. As an apostolic writer, he takes us on a journey through the gospels and allows history to become a teacher. The lessons from the epistles are classic. Only a true teacher and pastor can bring his readers into a private counseling session while instructing them in a fashion worthy of any seminary. I have worked alongside of the author for over thirty years in a ministry climate that generates such wisdom, knowledge, and discernment. And of all the books Dan Rhodes has written, this one expresses his true passion. He makes the Word become flesh.

Bishop Kirby Clements
Founder of the International Connection of Ministries, Atlanta, GA

Dan Rhodes is quite possibly the most gifted bible teacher I have ever listened to. His extensive scriptural knowledge along with his innovative communication skills makes him most effective in the ministry of imparting truth. Although his education and credentials fully qualify him for the ministry of the Word, it is his spiritual anointing that sets him apart. He is a man of impeccable character and stalwart resolve. This latest of his books is a masterful work of art that very effectively outlines the directives of God's word which points the way for all of us to safely navigate our own course of life successfully.

Pastor Richard E. Davis
Senior Pastor of Cove Bible Advance Ministries, Conyers, GA
and Liberty Church, Commerce, GA

Reading Pastor Dan Rhodes' book, *"Navigating Life With the Compass of God's Word"* is a journey into the beauties, complexities and treasures of the scriptures with a pastor, teacher, theologian whose passion for the Holy Spirit is rare on the earth today.

My wife and I have been friends with this dear man and his bride for almost 30 years. His biblical insights and counsel have often been the difference between life and death for us. I have been a pastor for 40 years and from that journey I know for a fact that the gift of God resident in Pastor Dan Rhodes as presented in this book will take anyone reading it more deeply into their destiny in the Kingdom of God than any other resource I can imagine.

Are you looking for a fluffy devotional? Well, keep looking because *"Navigating Life With the Compass of God's Word"* isn't fluff...it is Kingdom Come potent stuff!

Pastor Randy Dean
Senior Pastor of Living Word Chapel, Emerald, WI

In this body of work, Dan Rhodes has masterfully assimilated the ageless message of the Kingdom with astounding clarity, introducing a fresh perspective to a contemporary society. The believer who pursues this systematic and detailed path to understanding the role of the church and the individual believer in God's eternal plan will become empowered to fulfill their destiny.

Dan's many years of painstaking study and comprehensive writings on the subject places him among those master teachers possessing a sound theological grasp on this subject. This work will prove invaluable to the student seeking to unravel the mysteries surrounding this eternal truth while discovering their worth to the King and His Kingdom. I am grateful to God for depositing such a gift into the body of Christ for this generation and for the generations to come.

Bishop Nolan W. McCants
Founder of International Kingdom Alliance, Plainfield, Ill

Contents

The DRAMA, The MAP and The COMPASS 1

GENESIS
　Want a New Start? *How About a New Name Too?* 3

EXODUS
　Why Does it Take So LONG - *To Arrive at My Destiny?* 7

LEVITICUS
　Want Destiny? *Not Without a Restructured Life!* 11

NUMBERS
　Five Ways - *To Kiss Your Destiny Goodbye!* 15

DEUTERONOMY
　The Book Jesus Used - *To Defeat the Devil!* 19

JOSHUA
　The Book of Conquest - *Is Destiny Worth Fighting For?* 23

JUDGES
　I Didn't Think Living in My Destiny - *Would Be Like This!* ... 27

RUTH
　Discovering God's Unseen Hand - *In the Middle of a Crisis* ... 31

1 SAMUEL
　Your Child's Spirit - *What You May Not Know!* 35

2 SAMUEL
　When Your World Falls Apart - *Secrets to Greatness!* 39

1 KINGS
　How to Throw Away Your Heritage - *In Four Easy Steps!* ... 43

2 KINGS
　Life WITHOUT the Anointing - *WHERE Is the God of Elijah?* 47

1 CHRONICLES
My Spiritual DNA - *Who Am I Really?* 51

2 CHRONICLES
Fatal Counsel - *Who You Should NEVER Listen To!* 55

EZRA
God's Remnant - *Appalled at the Slow Cook of the Church!* .. 59

NEHEMIAH
Rebuilding Your Spiritual Life - *After it Falls Apart!* 63

ESTHER
Swimming With the Sharks - *Fish Food or a Fish Fry* 67

JOB
When Tragedy Strikes - *Finding Destiny Out of Disaster* 71

PSALMS
Unhappy? Angry? Afraid? *How Honest Can You Be With God?* 75

PROVERBS
God's Handbook of Common Sense - *Wisdom for Dummies!* 79

ECCLESIASTES
LIFE - *The ULTIMATE Reality Show!* 83

SONG OF SOLOMON
Up Close and Personal - *With God!* 87

ISAIAH
Got Prophecy? *Can't Reach Your Destiny Without It!* 91

JEREMIAH
Stepping Into the Heart of God - *Could You Handle It?* 95

LAMENTATIONS
Postmortem of a Destiny - *They Played the Fool!* 99

EZEKIEL
Feeling Trapped? *Don't Let Frustration Drown Out God!* ... 103

DANIEL
  Faith Crisis: Lord, if You Don't Show Up - *I'm Toast!* 107

HOSEA
  Does God Still Love Me - *After What I Did?* 111

JOEL
  In the Midst of Your Biggest Mess - *God Gives Hope!* 115

AMOS
  Amos WHO? *Why God Likes to Use Ordinary People* 119

OBADIAH
  I Don't Like This Book! *It Doesn't Make Me Happy!* 123

JONAH
  What if God Showed Mercy - *To the Person You Hate Most?* 127

MICAH
  The Remnant - *God's "Redemption Island" Survivors* 131

NAHUM
  Divine Justice - *When Bad Guys Get What's Coming to Them* 135

HABAKKUK
  How to Survive Life - *When Everything Is Falling Apart!* ... 139

ZEPHANIAH
  Do "Over-The-Top" Christians Annoy You? *Guess What Annoys God?* 143

HAGGAI
  God's Ultimate Solution When You Say, *"I Can't Do This!"* .. 147

ZECHARIAH
  Rebuilding a Destroyed Life - *Doing it God's Way* 151

MALACHI
  What Went Wrong?! *Postmortem of a Broken Religious System* 155

MATTHEW
Four Myths About Messiah - *Many Christians Still Believe Them Today!* 159

MARK
Two Famous "Losers" - *You'll Never Guess What They Did for God!* 163

LUKE
Jesus in 4-D and High-Definition - *What You'd Miss if You Didn't Read Luke* 167

JOHN
Last Man Standing! *How the Last Living Apostle Described Jesus* 171

ACTS
How Healthy Is Your Church? *Take This Test and Find Out!* 175

ROMANS
This Book Changed Christianity Forever. *It Can Transform You Too!* 179

1 CORINTHIANS
The Most Scandalous Church on the Planet! *Who Are They?* 183

2 CORINTHIANS
Marks of a True Calling of God - *It May Surprise You!* 187

GALATIANS
Slipping Back to the Old Ways Again? *Want a No-Guilt Solution?* 191

EPHESIANS
Where Most Pastors Won't Go - *When They Start Churches* 195

PHILIPPIANS
The Story Behind the Story - *What You'll Miss Without it!* 199

COLOSSIANS
New-Age Teaching in the Early Church! *The Colossian Heresy* ---- 203

1 THESSALONIANS
"Christ-Mass" Is What Happens - *When Christmas Is Over* -- 207

2 THESSALONIANS
Okay, So the Mayan Calendar Was Wrong. *When Will the World Really End?* ---- 211

1 TIMOTHY
You Say You Believe in God - *But Does God Believe in You?* ---- 215

2 TIMOTHY
Leaving a Legacy of Destiny - *For Your Great-Great-Grandchildren* ---- 219

TITUS
Starting a Church the WRONG Way! *The Flipside of Titus* ---- 223

PHILEMON
When Christians HATE One Another! *A Strategy for Reconciliation* ---- 227

HEBREWS
A New and Improved Christianity - *That's Called Mixture!* ---- 231

JAMES
YOU Call Yourself a CHRISTIAN? HA! *Straight Talk by Jesus' Brother!* ---- 235

1 PETER
Peter, Is That Really You? *How God's Grace Can Transform ANYBODY* ---- 239

2 PETER
Turning Your Worst Nightmare - *Into Your Greatest Victory!* ---- 243

1 JOHN
    The Enemy Within (Part 1): *"The Spirit of Antichrist!"* 247

2 JOHN
    The Enemy Within (Part 2): *"Gullible Christians!"* 251

3 JOHN
    The Enemy Within (Part 3): *"Control Freaks!"* 255

JUDE
    This Is a Real Game-Changer - *It'll Cause You to "Grow Up" in a Hurry!* 259

REVELATION
    The Great "Mystery" of God Is Finished! *But What Happens Next?* 263

EPILOGUE - *What Then Shall I Do?* 267

    How Can I Study "The Map" of God's Word? 269

    How Do I Follow the "Compass" of God's Spirit? 273

    How Does the Map and Compass Work Together to Help Me Reach My Destiny in Christ? 275

The Drama, The Map and The Compass

The Drama

Shakespeare may have had more insight than he realized. *"All the world's a stage; and all the men and women merely players."* The most celebrated English poet and pre-eminent dramatist of all times wrote of a fatalistic and pre-ordained view of human life. But what if he was on to a truism far greater than what he wrote. Life is most certainly a "Drama." But it's more than what Shakespeare thought. *It's the epic struggle of good versus evil. And **YOU** are playing out your life before an audience beyond your imagination...your family, your friends, your enemies, the angels in heaven, evil forces in the spiritual realm and even God Himself!*

Drama is all around us. It's in the choices we make, the people we befriend and the beliefs we embrace. But the most powerful drama took place eons ago. It's called, *"The Drama of the Kingdom of God."* It's the **Epic of the Ages**...set on the backdrop of eternity. It's the **Drama of Heaven and Earth**...of how God's glorious creation of peace, order and harmony was corrupted by an angelic insurrection led by Lucifer. It's **God's Strategy**...of how He corrects rebellion in the universe and restores all things to His original purpose. It's the **On-Going Struggle**...of good and evil played out on the stage of human experience. It's the **Story of Redemption and Restoration**...of how fallen humankind is saved from spiritual death and restored to their destiny of ruling and reigning with God on the earth. *And you, my friend, are in the middle of this drama...whether you know it or not!*

The Bible is filled with Drama. From Genesis to Revelation, people's lives are played out before your very eyes. They were people just like you and me. They entered the "stage" of life, made decisions, loved, laughed, cried, suffered and then the final curtain fell. *But along the way, God got involved in the journey with them. That's what The DRAMA is all about...God, You and the Choices you make.*

The Map and The Compass

When people discovered the Magnetic North Pole, it opened the entire world to be navigated. With a <u>map</u> and a <u>compass</u>, they could traverse through forests, over mountains and across oceans to arrive at their desired destination. But without it, they would be lost.

And so it is with life. God provides the "<u>Map</u>." It's the Christian Bible that reveals the epic story of God and His people. And He provides the "<u>Compass</u>"...His Holy Spirit. He's the One who guides you by opening your heart to His heart and causing the words of the Bible to come alive. Unless God's Spirit gently whispers in your heart, *"This is the way, walk in it,"* you will most certainly be lost (Is. 30:21). Unless God's Spirit applies the Word to your life, the Bible is just another book of literature. *These two, the Spirit and the written Word, work together as a Spiritual Navigation System for your life.* When you properly use God's Map and Compass, you can navigate through ALL of Life's Trials including Offenses, Betrayals, Relationship Struggles, Career and Health Challenges.

As much as most Christians want to read through the entire Bible and glean insights for life, it can become challenging. We all need a little help from those who have been trained in how to interpret Scripture in relevant terms. *Each book of the Bible has a central "Drama" (or Theme) of how God works with people.* It tells of how He guides, directs, corrects and commends them as they journey through life. It tells of how He warns people about life's pitfalls and leads them toward their divine Destiny in Him.

As you read through this book, you'll discover the Central Drama in each book of the Bible and Life-Navigational Insights with Practical Steps to achieve your purpose in Him. Listen carefully to the whispers of the Holy Spirit as you read. <u>Then take a few minutes to jot down what God's Spirit is saying to you at the end of each book.</u> *You'll be amazed at how He can lead you into His Destiny for your life.*

GENESIS

Want a New Start?
How About a New Name Too!

Okay, is this just another philosophical tip on how to keep New Year Resolutions or to start my life over again? *No, but this will revolutionize your life. Don't try to start over without this truth!*

- It's NOT another futile exercise in "Will-Power!"
- It NOT about Philosophy…It's about Redemption.
- It's all about Becoming Who You Really Are!

Want a New Start?
How About a New Name Too!

Tired of starting a "Brand New Life" each January...then realizing it's the "Same Old You" in February? With such idealistic grandeur we proclaim a "New Beginning" and then break our commitments with such shrinking resignation. Regardless of how hard you try, success with new beginnings is difficult to achieve. **But what if <u>God</u> gave you a "New Start"?** Let's see what the Book of Genesis has to say about this.

Genesis is the "Book of Beginnings." Within the pages of this first book of the Bible we discover:

- <u>The Beginning of the World</u>. The earth and every living creature came into existence at God's command, not by some scientist's theory of random cosmic events (Gen. 1).

- <u>God's First Command to You</u>. God's original assignment to humankind (that's you and me) was to represent His righteous rule on earth. We were created as God's delegated authorities to exercise dominion over anything that opposes His purposes (Gen. 1:26-28; 2:15-17).

- <u>The Beginning of a Dysfunctional World</u>. Sin didn't start in the Garden...it began in heaven! Angels that rose up against God and were cast to the earth bringing with them spiritual darkness and disorder (Is. 14:12-17; Rev. 12:7-9; Gen. 3:1-5). Our failure to rule over Satan's deception caused us to lose our relationship with God and forfeit our Destiny. Futility, Pain, Brokenness and Corruption became humanity's inheritance (Gen. 3).

- <u>The Beginning of Your Restored Destiny</u>. All appeared to be lost until God revealed Satan's final end...crushed by the

"Seed" of the woman! That Seed is Jesus. In Him, humankind can be restored back to God as His <u>Redeemed Representatives</u> in the earth (Gen. 3:15).

Genesis Also Records the First Account of God Changing a Person's Name.

The meaning of your name connects you to the character and identity your parents hoped you would achieve. However, in Genesis, God changed the names of three people: Abram to **Abraham** (Gen. 17:5-9), Sarai to **Sarah** (Gen. 17:15-16) and Jacob to **Israel** (Gen. 32:24-30). **When God changes a name, it brings a <u>New Sense of Belonging</u> and a <u>New Identity</u> for a <u>New Destiny</u> in Him.** *(Read the stories of these three people and you'll see how their lives changed.)*

So, What Can You Learn from the Book of Genesis to Help You Navigate Life?

1. **A New Start Isn't "New"...It's a Restored Destiny!** That which Adam lost in the Garden, Jesus restored to you through His Redemptive work on Calvary's Cross. He restored your relationship with God and your Original Assignment: **You are called to represent His righteous rule on the earth!**

2. **When God Restores Your Destiny, He Gives You a "New Name!"** No, your new name isn't written on paper nor is it recorded in your county court house. God writes it in your **<u>HEART</u>** and records it in **<u>HEAVEN</u>**! *(Read Rev. 2:17 and 3:12.)* That new name removes the shame of your past and gives you a New Identity and a New Reputation. It awakens within you the original assignment of God. **You now bear the name of the One who redeemed you..Jesus (Acts 9:15)!**

3. **So, Don't Begin Your New Life with "Resolutions"...Begin It With "Restoration!"** You have been reinstated by the Savior to

change the dysfunctional world where you live. Do you see injustice? Do something about it! Do you see hopelessness? Give people hope in Jesus! Do you see chaos? Bring God's righteous order! Use the gifts and calling God gave you to make a difference in people's lives. It's not about trying to change your life; it's yielding to the power of God's Spirit to walk in what He already gave you...a Restored Destiny and New Name. It's Christ in <u>YOU</u>! (Gal. 2:20)

<u>What is God's Spirit Saying to Me...</u>
As I Navigate Life According To Genesis

EXODUS

Why Does it Take So LONG...
To Arrive at My Destiny?

Know anyone who's struggling with their Identity and Purpose in life? How about someone who's frustrated because they haven't found it yet? *This Teaching is for Them...and for You!*

- Why is God so SLOW about bringing me to my Destiny?
- And by the way...What is Destiny?
- What does the Book of Exodus have to do with all of this?

Why Does it Take So LONG...
To Arrive at My Destiny?

Some have found it. Others aren't sure. But for many, trying to arrive at their God-given Destiny is like searching for the illusive pot of gold at the rainbow's end. As soon as you reach where you thought it was...it's gone! Then it reappears again just over the next hill. **Perhaps Destiny is something different than what most people think.** Let's see what insight the Book of Exodus can give us.

The word "Exodus" literally means the **"Road Out."** It's the Book of Deliverance telling the familiar story of how God delivered Israel **"Out Of"** Egyptian bondage and **Into** God's Destiny for their lives. It tracks how one family (Jacob and his 12 sons) grew into the great nation of Israel. It's how God led them into His promises...the "Promised Land." Here are some highlights of this action packed book:

- In Genesis we learned that God created and gifted all human beings with divine distinction and purpose to represent His righteousness rule on earth (Gen. 1:26-28). However, their destiny was derailed by Satan who deceived them and enslaved all humankind in sin (Gen. 3).

- Exodus is the On-going Drama of that enslavement. It's the story of how God delivered His people <u>Out Of</u> Egypt's control and the false religion of the land (a type of satanic bondage).

- Hearing their cries, God raised up a deliverer (Moses) and anointed him with great power to confront and break the "System" (Egypt) that **held them in pagan bondage for 400 years.**

- But instead of taking them the short route to Canaan *(less than a month's travel)*, God led them through the Wilderness *(the*

LONG way). Why? Because their destiny was more than a piece of land in the Middle East...it was a relationship with the Living God! Forty years later, they finally entered Canaan.

So, How Does The Exodus Story Help You Navigate Your Destiny in God?

1. **First of All, Your Destiny Isn't a Place.** It's living in a personal relationship with God and according to His wondrous plan. Destiny is a "Calling" that enhances who you are and what you can do best.

2. **Identify Your "Egypt."** What is God delivering you from? "Egypt" is anything that enslaves you and hinders God's ultimate intentions for your life. You have a Deliverer greater than Moses who leads you into God's freedom. It's Jesus! Follow Him and you'll truly be free (Luke 4:18-19).

3. **Be Patient!** The "Road Out" of bondage takes time. Like Israel, you've been assimilated into the world's "System" that ignores the one True God, glorifies human achievement and oppresses the helpless. *You can quickly get out of Egypt...but it takes a life-time to get Egypt out of you!*

4. **The Farther Down the Road You Are, The Harder It Is To Return To Egypt.** The shortest route to Canaan was heavily guarded and Israel was no match for battle hardened warriors. God knew that at the first taste of war, they would return to the oppressors they prayed to be delivered from (Ex. 13:17-18)! It takes a LONG time to get a LONG way from your bondage.

5. **God Is Teaching You To Trust Him.** Trust isn't automatic...it takes hardships, failures, victories and a life-time of experiences to know that God is with you in the good times and the bad. Trust requires humility. The proud heart will

never trust God. Wilderness experiences cure our human pride (Deut. 8:2-5).

And that, my friend, is why it takes so <u>LONG</u> to arrive at your Destiny. But here's the real truth. If you're on this amazing journey with God, you're already well into your Destiny. Why? Because you're following His "Map" and being led by His "Compass." And what's your Destiny? It's a deeper relationship with the Lord and a closer walk with Him in every part of your life.

<u>What is God's Spirit Saying to Me...</u>
As I Navigate Life According To Exodus

_____

_____

_____

_____

_____

_____

_____

_____

_____

_____

_____

LEVITICUS

Want Destiny?
Not Without a Re-Structured Life!

Many Christians ignore or just skip over the Old Testament (especially Leviticus) because they think it's totally outdated by their New Covenant in Jesus. You'll be surprised to learn how WRONG they are!

- Leviticus is just a book about Jewish laws that don't concern Christians...Right?
- If I'm a Christian, God guarantees that I'll walk in my Destiny...Right?
- God's Grace will always keep me from losing my Destiny...Right?

Want Destiny?
Not Without a Re-Structured Life!

No hymn has ever been written that beckons the sinner to Christ more than these inspired words: *"Just as I am...Thou wilt receive; wilt welcome, pardon, cleanse, relieve. Because Thy promise I believe; O Lamb of God, I come! I come!"* With tears coursing down our faces, we confess our total depravity and receive God's unmerited love and acceptance. BUT <u>AFTER</u> receiving His saving grace, don't think you can please God by remaining "Just As You Used To Be!" That's what Israel discovered in the Book of Leviticus. **Unless you discover this truth as well, your Destiny will slip through your fingers like sand!**

Leviticus derives its name from the Levitical Priesthood to whom God gave the sacred assignment of ministering the rituals of redemption. After 400 years in pagan captivity, God was **REMOVING** the stain of Egypt out of their hearts and **RE-STRUCTURING** their lives. Here's what God taught them:

- <u>Holiness</u>. It's being in God's league...separated from sin and set apart for His righteous purposes (Lev. 11:44-45). That, my friend, can't happen until your sins are cleansed through the blood of atonement. It also means renouncing evil, resisting sin and doing the things that please the Lord.

- <u>Justice</u>. It's doing what's right according to God's standards. It's acting in fairness without partiality and submitting to the righteous government of God. It's how God requires us to treat one another and it's how God deals with us (Lev. 19:32-37; Ps. 89:14).

- <u>Mercy</u>. The focal point of the Holy of Holies was the Mercy Seat. It was the covering for the Ark of the Covenant, without which salvation would be impossible (Lev. 16:11-16). Mercy flows from God's love and His compassion for the pitiful plight of fallen humankind. He knows we deserve punishment for our sins, yet He knows we're trapped and unable to keep from sinning.

In reading Leviticus, you may grow weary with the never-ending laws...laws for bringing sacrifices to God, laws for the priests, laws for the atonement, dietary laws, cleansing laws, morality laws and civil laws for how people should treat one another! *"So, what does this have to do with my Destiny?"* you may ask.

1. **Don't Kid Yourself...Salvation Is NOT a Free Ticket to Your Destiny!** Just as Israel needed God's help to get Egypt's world system out of their hearts, so do you. God's Laws are like a "schoolmaster" that **Re-Structures** your life so you'll know how to live in His presence (Gal. 3:19-27). But, like Nadab and Abihu who rejected God's ways, you too can be disqualified from your Destiny (Lev. 10:1-4). Even the great Apostle Paul understood that sober reality (1 Cor. 9:24-27).

2. **It's NOT Legalism or Sloppy Grace!** To walk in your Destiny doesn't return you to bondage to the Law nor does it mean you can throw away the Law. Faith in Christ stirs your heart for good works...not trying to <u>earn</u> God's favor but it's because you <u>have</u> His favor that you want to please Him (James 2:14-24).

3. **Even Jesus Requires You to Change Your Behavior (John 8:11-12; Matt. 7:16-27)!** Good behavior won't save you, but when God redeems you, the fruit of your life should show it. Paul admonishes all Christians to "lay aside the old self" and "put on the new" (Eph. 4:17-32).

Some may say, *"I know I'm a Christian and I love Jesus, but I still sin and fall short of God's intentions. Does that mean I'll lose my Destiny?"* Well, **it all depends!** If you don't discard the truth of Leviticus <u>AND</u> if you walk in the light of Jesus, darkness in your life becomes obvious. As you recognize sin, confess it and allow Jesus to cleanse you (1 John 1:5-10; 2:1-17). But, if you continually ignore His Re-Structuring Work and Cleansing Light, you may be moving dangerously close to apostasy...falling away from the Living God (Heb. 3:12; 6:4-6). ***But by following God's Map and Compass, you can be assured that it will never happen to you.***

What is God's Spirit Saying to Me...
As I Navigate Life According To Leviticus

NUMBERS

Five Ways...
To Kiss Your Destiny Goodbye!

Have you ever watched people throw their futures away and you didn't know how to warn them? *The Principles taught in the Book of Numbers may save their lives...and maybe even <u>yours</u> too!*

- Five fatal errors that cost 600,000 people their futures and their lives!
- Don't disregard negative examples. Learn from them and live!
- Only two people did it the right way. What was the secret of their success?

Five Ways...
To Kiss Your Destiny Goodbye!

"For of all sad words of tongue or pen, the saddest of these: 'It Might Have Been!'" These poignant words of John Greenleaf Whittier, American poet and abolitionist, are as relevant today as they were in 1854 when he wrote them. Every person who has experienced regret over lost opportunities knows all too well these sorrowful emotions. Whether it's your personal failure or the horror of seeing another's life's work and Destiny collapse in a heap of rubble, grief over what "Might Have Been" seems unbearable. After 40 years of suffering the consequences of failure and lost opportunities in the wilderness, Israel epitomized Whittier's poem.

Numbers is the story of Israel's wanderings in the wilderness. Scholars gave this book its traditional name, "Numbers," because it contains a record of the great census of Israel's people. But the Hebrews gave it a more appropriate name: **"In the Wilderness."** The real tragedy of the book is this: **Every person over the age of 20 <u>died</u> in the wilderness! They failed to obtain the Destiny God intended (Num. 14:26-30).** This is how they "Kissed Their Destiny Goodbye"...and this is how it could happen to you!

1. **Complain Against God's Provisions (Num. 11:1-7).** God doesn't always lead you down easy paths and sumptuous living. Hardships build spiritual character. Yet He provides what you <u>NEED</u>...not what you <u>WANT</u> (Deut. 8:2-10). *God views complaints as ingratitude and rebellion!*

2. **Give Up When You Hit a Brick Wall (Num. 13:25-33).** If you focus on the obstacles and your inabilities rather than on God's power to fulfill His promises, fear and insecurity will overtake your heart. *When God says "Go" and you Don't, He views that as rebellion and unbelief!*

3. **Toxic Emotions When God Chooses Someone Else** (Num. 16). Jealousy and Resentment are lethal! Korah, cousin of Moses and Aaron, led a rebellion against them. He felt that <u>he</u>, not Aaron, should have been the High Priest. *God dealt swiftly and Korah died in the wilderness!*

4. **Mix Personal Frustrations with Ministry** (Num. 20:1-12; Deut. 3:25-27). Moses was fed up with the people's belligerent complaints against him and God. *But when he took matters into his own hands, it cost him his Destiny. God disqualified Moses from entering the Promised Land!*

5. **Failure to Conquer Your Personal Demons** (Num. 33:51-56). For Israel, it was allowing their enemies to live in the land God gave them. For you and me, it's allowing anything to remain in our lives that draw us away from God. *It'll trip you up and steal your Destiny from you!*

Some may ask, *"Why are you so negative? Can't you just tell me how to achieve my Destiny?"* I wouldn't be true to God's word if I didn't give you these warnings. But here's the positive side:

1. **Learn From Israel's Mistakes!** Make note of how they failed. Then guard your heart against those fatal errors. Reverse each of the five points above and you'll be on a path that protects your Destiny.

2. **Follow the Example of Joshua and Caleb.** Of the 600,000 people over the age of 20, only <u>TWO</u> people made it to their Destiny...Joshua and Caleb! Why? *1- They Radically Believed God (Num. 13:27-30); 2- They publically stood against the deceived majority who chose to disbelieve God (Num. 14:2-10); 3- They Fully Followed the Lord (Num. 14:22-24).*

How can you **Navigate Life** and **Protect Your Destiny** according to the Drama in the Book of Numbers? Learn from lessons you just read. Remember, Forewarned is Forearmed!

What is God's Spirit Saying to Me...
As I Navigate Life According To Numbers

DEUTERONOMY

The Book Jesus Used...
To Defeat the Devil!

Spiritual Warfare is an electrifying concept. But many may be misinformed and confused about fighting the unseen forces of Satan. ***Few know what Jesus REALLY did to defeat the devil when He met him face to face!***

- What does "Spiritual Warfare" really mean?
- Satan used his best strategy against Jesus. What was it?
- What's so special about Deuteronomy and why did Jesus use that book?

The Book Jesus Used...
To Defeat the Devil!

Spiritual Warfare is not what some people think. It's **NOT** an aggravating co-worker, a bounced check or a power outage in the middle of a church service. And you can't stop the devil by screaming rebukes with your angry words. Spiritual Warfare is *"standing firm against the schemes of the devil"* (Eph. 6:11). The Greek word for "schemes" is where we get the English word "Method"...a systematic strategy for attaining an objective. **The devil's strategy is to <u>STOP</u> you from becoming who God created you to be. He wants to <u>STOP</u> you from doing what God calls you to do. In other words, he's after your <u>Destiny</u>!** How did Jesus stop Satan when he attacked His Destiny? He quoted the Word of God...from the Book of Deuteronomy!

"Deuteronomy" means "Second Law"...the second time Moses gave God's Law to Israel. After 40 years in the wilderness, Moses' life was coming to an end. He had one last chance to give the next generation what the older had rejected...God's Law! The Law is more than Ten Commandments; it's the will of God found in the entirety of His Written Word. It's the **<u>STANDARD</u>** by which He orders society and judges good and evil. It's His divine authority that "arrests" (stops) those who challenge His purposes.

Matthew chapter four records the astounding confrontation between Jesus and the devil...face to face! This was Satan's big chance to derail the Son of God's earthly ministry. **He threw at Jesus the very thing that we all want...a <u>shortcut</u> to our Destiny!** *Interestingly, Deuteronomy rehearses the story of Israel's test in the wilderness (Deut. 8:2). Jesus quoted from Deuteronomy in order to pass **His** test in the wilderness!* Look at **Satan's strategy** and how Jesus shut him down! ***Listen as Satan challenges Jesus. It's the same way he challenges you and me!***

1. **Go Ahead...Use Your God-Given Gift For Personal Gain. *You Deserve It!*** (Matt. 4:2-3). This shortcut offered Jesus the chance to prove who He was destined to be...by satisfying the appetites of His flesh! Jesus countered Satan's temptation with, *"It Is Written!"* In other words, God's Word is "The STANDARD" I live by!" Then He quoted from Deut. 8:2-3 (Israel's wilderness experience): *"My life-source is more than temporal things. I live by God and His Word!"*

2. **Oh, You Want To Play The "Scripture Game?" I Can Quote The Bible Too...*Out of Context That Is!*** (Matt. 4:5-7). Satan went to the next level of deception: **Twisting scripture to make it say what you want it to say!** This approach always works for those who have a shallow knowledge of God's Word. Jesus used the whole counsel of "The STANDARD" to refute Satan. He quoted from Deut. 6:14-17: *"I will NOT challenge God's character with a presumptuous belief system!"*

3. **Okay, I Will Fulfill Your Destiny For You...*And You Won't Have To Go To The Cross!*** The devil was at the top of his game on this one. Jesus came to earth to restore people and bring the rebellious kingdoms of the world back to God's rule (Rev. 11:15). Satan offered Him those kingdoms without the need for His redemptive sacrifice. The only problem is that a "Cross-less" Destiny doesn't redeem you and you're still serving the devil! Again, Jesus went to "The STANDARD" of God's Word in Deut. 6:12-15. *"My assignment comes from God...NOT from you!"*

So, what does all this have to do with you and your Destiny? Your Destiny is more than your job, your marital status or where you live. *Your Destiny is who you ARE and what you DO to glorify God. It means standing against evil in your job, your marriage and where you live.* Satan has no new tricks...he just finds new people to deceive. Study the three strategies of Satan above and identify how he's working in your life. Then follow Jesus' example. Use the entire **STANDARD** of God's Word to defeat Satan's strategies. But remember...once you stop him, he'll be back to try again and again and again (Luke 4:13)!

What is God's Spirit Saying to Me...
As I Navigate Life According To Deuteronomy

JOSHUA

The Book of Conquest
Is Your Destiny Worth Fighting For?

Pastors have unique callings...we see lives from beginning to end. We walk with people and warn them of life's pitfalls. *Tragically, some let their Destinies slip away...even without a fight!*

- What causes people to fight for certain things and let other things drop by the wayside?
- Four strategies to keep you from losing your Destiny.
- Will you fight for your Destiny? A Reality Check!

The Book of Conquest
Is Your Destiny Worth Fighting For?

"Anything Worth Having Is Worth Fighting For!" Everyone from Thomas Jefferson to your High School Teacher has been credited with this motivational zinger. Here's another way of saying it: *"Whatever you DON'T value, you WON'T fight to keep!"* So what do you value and what is worth fighting or even dying for? For patriots, it's their nation and way of life. For young men or women in love, it's their relationships. For drivers who think they're "Kings of the Road," they'll foolishly fight (even die) over a parking place or a bruised ego when they're cut off in traffic. **But for Joshua and Israel, the prize worth fighting for was the Promise of God and their Divine Destiny!**

Joshua was the man chosen by God to lead Israel after Moses died. The book, named after him, records how he crossed the River Jordan and fought to inherit the land God promised to give them. It only takes about 1½ hours to read it, but it took 50 years for them to live it. It's the story of a valiant people who followed God and won victories in the face of overwhelming odds. But it's also the story of some who failed because of selfish desires (Josh. 7) and gullibility (Josh. 9). **Take note of the following navigational strategies found in Joshua's book...they just might keep you from losing your Destiny!**

1. **Joshua Wasn't Just Doing His Own Thing...He Was Following A Divine Destiny!** There is a tendency for the next generation to discard the values of previous generations. They want something fresh and new. "Fresh and New" is okay as long as the foundation is God who continues His work from generation to generation (Ps. 90:1-2). Destiny is both personal and trans-generational. *A wise generation discovers God's timeless work and makes it relevant.*

2. **News Flash...God's Promises Aren't Free!** When God gives a promise it doesn't mean you can sit back, munch potato chips and watch the blessings roll in! Paul spoke of *"Fighting the good fight of faith"* (1 Tim. 6:12). This has the connotation of an athlete competing for a prize with intense energy. ***God's promises are conditional upon your actions (Jer. 18:7-10; Matt. 7:21-27).***

3. **There's a Powerful Enemy Scheming to Steal Your Destiny from You!** Just as Joshua ran into walled cities, strong armies and giants in the Promised Land, so will you in the land of your Destiny. Like a prowling lion, the devil is seeking to devour you and God's purpose for your life (1 Pet. 5:8-9). Learn how to resist him so that you won't be disqualified from inheriting God's promises (James 4:7-10; 1 Cor. 9:23-27).

4. **Finally, There Is NO Substitute For a Consecrated Life!** Joshua was about to lead his nation into war. But instead of telling them to put on armor and sharpen swords, he commanded them to consecrate themselves to God (Josh. 3:5). That meant to separate themselves from anything that separates them from God! Why? Because he knew they couldn't win this kind of battle without God! The quest for your Destiny in God is spiritual. Without Him, you've already lost it!

Now to the Question: **"Is Your Destiny Worth Fighting For?"** Here's a Reality Check! ***Remember, your ultimate Destiny is God!*** A personal relationship with His Son, Jesus, connects you to God and His purposes for your life. Who you **ARE** in Him and what you **DO** for Him is God's call on your life. If you don't value these things, you won't fight to maintain a personal relationship with God. You'll sin and not feel godly sorrow. You'll justify wrong attitudes and not seek forgiveness. You'll get offended and walk away from God, His church and your fellowship with other Christians. Then you may die without Christ in your life and lose eternity with Him. So, I'll ask the question again..."Is Your Destiny Worth Fighting For?" *If it is, then let God's Map and His Compass lead you into your "Promised Land."*

What is God's Spirit Saying to Me...
As I Navigate Life According To Joshua

JUDGES

I Didn't Think Living in My Destiny... Would Be Like This!

Do you know someone who lives in a cycle of Broken Promises to God? They don't know WHY they keep repeating failure. *The lesson learned from the book of Judges is for them...and maybe for you too!*

- What did Israel **Fail** to do that could have stopped their cycle?
- Here it is...the **Pattern** that most of us fall into!
- Three ways you can **Break** the cycle and move from sinful habits to a righteous life!

I Didn't Think Living in My Destiny... Would Be Like This!

"I thought when I finally discovered my Destiny, it would be smooth sailing! But instead...things got worse! What's going on here?" In our idyllic minds, we envision our "Land of Destiny" like a Divine Theme Park where every day is good times, fun and fulfillment. Unfortunately this couldn't be farther from the truth. When Israel entered into their Promised Land, it was battle after battle until they finally took possession of the land. However, in all their victories they failed to do one "LITTLE" thing. **They didn't drive out ALL their enemies!** The Book of Judges tells their sad story!

The best way to describe Judges is like this: **It was a 400 year Roller Coaster Ride of Broken Promises to God!** Joshua was dead; there was no central leadership; and the people were left to serve God by themselves. So what happened? *"Every man did what was right in his own eyes" (Judg. 17:6).* It was a recurring real-life nightmare... generation after generation after generation! And this was why:

1. **Demonic Temptations Were Too Strong for Them.** Because they didn't eradicate the influence of pagan lifestyles, God's people became just like their enemies...corrupt and vile! They exchanged their God, who delivered them from Egypt, for the false gods and religions of the land (Rom. 1:20-32).

2. **Sin Brought Consequences.** God's Standard (His Word) is like a Guard Rail that protects us from dangers. When we choose to "play" outside the Guard Rail, we can fall off the cliff! When Israel became like those who hated God, He had to back away and let their enemies rule over their lives!

3. **Then They Cried to God for Help!** Mercifully, God raised up Judges...champions who delivered them from the oppression

of their enemies. Mighty Judges like Deborah (Judg. 4-5), Gideon (Judg. 6-8) and Samson (Judg. 13-16) led them in battle and the people would return to God.

4. **But They Slipped Back Into Their Old Ways!** When a Judge died, the people who had promised to serve God, returned to their old patterns of sin and corruption. And the Roller Coaster Ride continued: *Sin; Consequences; Cries for Help; Deliverance; Broken Promises!*

Does this pattern look familiar? If we're honest, all of us would cry out, *"OMG (that's slang for Oh My Gosh)...You just described MY life! How can I get off this Nightmare Ride?"* Consider this:

1. **Your Walk with God Isn't a Casual Stroll...You're in a WAR Against Evil (Gen. 6:9-12)!** Your Ultimate Destiny is to become and act like the person God created you to be. You're a warrior against evil in your life and in the lives of others. That's why Faith is called the good "Fight" (1 Tim. 6:12).

2. **Don't Give the Devil an Opportunity (Eph. 4:22-27)!** Read God's command and His warning in **Deut. 7:1-6.** Israel failed to do this...and so have we! Ask God to show you the ungodly influences in your life that must be destroyed...*the things that pull you back into the "old ways" of life and bring you down (Heb. 12:1-2).* Whatever it takes, get rid of them (Gal. 5:24-25)!

3. **But Here's the GOOD NEWS!** Where both Israel and we failed...Jesus didn't! He was victorious over sin and temptation (Heb. 4:15-16). And even more...He gives His victory and His righteousness to those who trust in Him (2 Cor. 5:21; Rom. 3:26)! *Listen closely, my friend, only Jesus can stop the cycle of sin in your life (John 8:3-12; 1 John 2:1-2)!*

Navigating Life With God's Compass

So, what does the book of Judges have to do with Navigating Your Life? Everything! *God's Map of Judges shows you life's pitfalls that you must avoid. And the Compass of God's Spirit points you toward your Destiny in Him. Now all you have to do is believe God and follow His directions!*

What is God's Spirit Saying to Me...
As I Navigate Life According To Judges

RUTH

Discovering God's Unseen Hand... In the Middle of a Crisis

Have you ever wondered where God was when you were in the middle of a heartbreaking crisis? Why couldn't you see Him? *This teaching will open your eyes to see what most can never see!*

- What are crises and where do they come from?
- You'll never guess where God was during Ruth's crisis!
- How can you **"See"** God's **"Unseen"** hand?

Discovering God's Unseen Hand...
In the Middle of a Crisis

A Crisis is a Turning Point in Life. Some crises are unprovoked while others may be self-inflicted. Lack of preplanning, foresight and preventive action can ruin your day, a vacation or even your career. However, severe weather, a sudden illness or a traffic accident can strike without warning. Regardless of the cause, when a crisis hits it's an <u>opportunity</u> to <u>turn your life around</u> with good decisions. *But what you CAN'T see is how God is walking with you and helping you with your decisions.*

The book of Ruth opens with one crisis after another. It begins with a devastating famine that forced Naomi, her husband and two sons to leave their homeland and live in a pagan nation. Then tragedy struck...Naomi's husband died! On the heels of that nightmare, her sons married pagan women. Then tragedy struck again. Both Naomi's sons died and she was left alone in a foreign land with two pagan daughters-in-law. What happened next was beyond Ruth's ability to <u>see</u> or to <u>know</u>. *God's unseen hand was at work even when she couldn't see it!* Look what was happening behind the scenes in Ruth's crisis:

1. **Ruth Chose to Believe in Naomi's God Rather Than Cultural Preferences and Personal Gain (Ruth 1:8-17).** With the security of her husband gone, Ruth could have chosen the easy road...remain with her people, remarry within her culture and serve the gods she grew up with. But she chose to go with Naomi instead. *What she <u>couldn't see</u> was the One True God who was tugging at her heart and directing her steps!*

2. **Ruth Trusted in God's Providential Favor (Ruth 2:1-3).** When she and Naomi arrived back in Judah, what was she going to do? No money. No food. No friends. Ruth didn't know how... but deep within her heart she believed her new God would

take care of her. *What she <u>couldn't see</u> was God's long-ranged plan for her life...a plan that included Boaz, their children and their great-grandchild!*

3. **Ruth Followed Wise Counsel (Ruth 3:1-5).** When Naomi recognized the providential hand of God at work, she gave Ruth wisdom on how to approach Boaz with grace, humility and integrity. *What she <u>didn't know</u> was that Boaz would never have responded to anything less. It was the counsel of God working through Naomi to give her favor with Naomi's relative, Boaz.*

4. **Ruth Requested "Redemption" from Boaz (Ruth 3:6-11).** The word for "kinsman" in Ruth 3:9 is actually "Kinsman-Redeemer"...meaning "to redeem a kin from difficulty or danger." Listen to Ruth's request to Boaz as translated by the Message Bible, *"take me under your protecting wing."* *What she <u>didn't know</u> was that she would bear a son named Obed; who would become the father of Jesse; who would become the father of David the Great King! And from the lineage of King David would be born the greatest of all Kings..Jesus, the REDEEMER of the world!*

And so, my friend, your life may be similar to Ruth's drama. You can't see God's hand in your life...until you look backward. *Then you will discover that God was with you during the most difficult times in your life...helping you to navigate your Destiny in Him!*

1. Do you sense a slight "tug" in your heart drawing you nearer to God and His love for you? **Yield to His unseen hand, my friend! That's the work of His Holy Spirit.**

2. Have you run out of answers in life and don't know where to turn? **Trust God's providential grace. He has a long-ranged plan better than you can possibly imagine!**

3. Do you hear wise counsel from someone more mature in God than you? Follow it...especially if it has the ingredients of grace, humility and integrity!

4. Finally, do you need your life redeemed? **Ask Jesus, The REDEEMER,** to *"take you under His protecting wing."* He will redeem both your life and your Destiny in Him!

What is God's Spirit Saying to Me...
As I Navigate Life According To Ruth

1 SAMUEL

Your Child's Spirit
What You May Not Know!

Years ago when my wife and I were young parents, we read book after book on how to raise a Christian family. *They were excellent...but they didn't tell us this:*

- How old do your children have to be before they can hear from God?
- When do your children develop a purpose for their lives?
- What can you do as a parent or a grandparent to help navigate your children's Destinies in God?

Your Child's Spirit
What You May Not Know!

"If I knew <u>Then</u> what I know <u>Now</u>...!" This haunting truism is quoted, made into songs and stirs regretful hearts to wish they had done things differently in life. It speaks to knowledge and wisdom that only comes from making wrong choices, missed opportunities and suffering the consequences of being naïve. This can be especially true when it comes to the raising of children. **If only we knew <u>then</u> what we know <u>now</u>, perhaps we could have been better parents.** The book of First Samuel records an astonishing story that stirred my heart to write this navigational insight. It's the story of a very young child and his Destiny in God.

Samuel was Israel's last judge before they transitioned to a monarchy. But Samuel was more than a judge...he was a prophet! He anointed kings and organized the newly forming kingdom of Israel. **The powerful reality of this story was Samuel's age when God called him...he was a mere child!** Equally as powerful was what the Lord said to him. **He revealed things far beyond his physical maturity level.** God told him He was about to bring judgment on the old priest who was raising Samuel (1 Sam. 3)!

So what do you learn from this story? **A young child's human spirit can be touched by God's Spirit...regardless of age.** Look what else you may not know about your children:

1. They Have Callings and Destinies in God...*Even Before They're Born!* If you don't believe it, read **Jer. 1:5**. Then read about David in **Ps. 22:9-10**. If you still don't believe it, read about Paul in **Gal. 1:15-16**. Finally, read **Rom. 8:28-30**. *Raise your children with the knowledge that God knows them...even <u>better</u> than you do!*

2. They Can <u>Respond</u> To God...*Even as Infants and Even in the Womb!* Now this is mind-boggling! John the Baptist <u>responded</u> to his Destiny and was even <u>filled with the Holy Spirit</u> while he was yet unborn (Luke 1:15, 41, 44)! Here's why: The human spirit is the likeness and character of God within a person (Gen. 1:26; 2:7). It's the Holy Spirit's "portal" into the soul (Prov. 20:27). ***Children can respond to God's presence regardless of their physical maturity!***

3. The Devil Knows These Things...*Even <u>Before</u> You Do!* That's why Satan tried to destroy the infant Moses (Ex. 1:22) and the child Jesus (Matt. 2:13-16). And he'll do anything to derail (or kill) your children's Destiny in God before they can become a force against him (Rev. 12:4, 17).

Now that you know these truths, what can you do to help navigate your children's Destinies? ***Even if you didn't know these things when you were raising your children, it's not too late for your grandchildren!***

1. Do What Samuel's Mother Did. <u>GIVE</u> Your Children To The Lord (1 Sam. 1:10-11). It's one thing to go through the motions of a church dedication service. It's a totally different matter to intently pray and completely trust God with your children's lives. ***God honors that kind of prayer!***

2. Surround Them With God's Presence. Speak often to your children about the Lord. Let them hear worshipful music. Let them hear your prayers and the prayers of anointed men and women. ***God is working His purposes into your child...even before birth (Ps. 139:13-16)!***

3. Become a Guardian Over Their Impressionable Lives. This means naturally and spiritually. Pray fervently against the wicked plans of people and powers of evil who want to "steal, kill and destroy." ***Not only are you protecting their lives...but***

also their Destinies that may impact thousands of lives and Destinies in the future!

What is God's Spirit Saying to Me...
As I Navigate Life According To 1 Samuel

2 SAMUEL

When Your World Falls Apart
Secrets to Greatness!

What can you do when life begins to crumble before your eyes? Some grow bitter; some accuse God and some give up. *But King David did something totally different. Check it out!*

- How can I be "Great" with the problems like I have?
- What if I'm totally at fault...Now what can I do?
- Five Secrets to David's Greatness...and yours too!

When Your World Falls Apart
Secrets to Greatness!

"The ultimate measure of a man is not where he stands in moments of comfort and convenience, but where he stands at times of challenge and controversy." That was Martin Luther King's stirring declaration during America's Civil Rights struggle in the mid-1960s. Difficult times try the mettle of men's souls. Whether it's a crisis in a nation, contention in a family, a melt-down in a career or the collapse of personal morals, *God takes note of how you handle life's tragedies...both in yourself and in others!*

The Bible doesn't gloss over sin...it reveals the ugliness and tragic consequences of foolish behavior. Samuel's second book tells how David rose to the throne of Israel but then failed morally in his personal life. Samuel openly reveals the good, the bad and the ugly about our beloved King David. Saul, the first king, disqualified himself with pride, presumption and witchcraft. And David was no "angel" either! *If you think YOU'RE having a bad life, try David's on for size.*

- <u>Adultery and Murder</u>! Not only did David commit adultery with Bathsheba, she got pregnant and he couldn't cover it up. So David had her husband killed! Then the child died (2 Sam. 11-12).

- <u>Family Incest and Murder</u>! David's daughter, Tamar, was violated by her half-brother, Amnon. For revenge, Absalom, another of David's sons, killed Amnon (2 Sam. 13).

- <u>Betrayal by Absalom</u>! Absalom was David's favorite son. But he led a rebellion against his dad and drove him out of the palace. Then Absalom was brutally killed by the Commander of David's army (2 Sam. 15-18).

Yet in the midst of his Fame and Folly, David loved the Lord! And God loved David...so much so that He declared in Acts 13:22, *"I have found David...a man after My own heart"!* My friend, don't follow David's sin! But if you want to be great in God's heart, look at what impressed the Lord about David:

1. **He Had Passion for God.** Read a few of David's psalms to get a glimpse of his inward zeal for the Lord (Ps. 18:1-3). And he wasn't afraid to declare it with his actions (2 Sam. 6:14-16) and his writings. *Passion for God is our human response to His passion for us!* (1 John 3:1)

2. **He Had Honest and Open Talks with God.** When David was hurting or afraid, he openly spoke to the Lord about it. Yet in the midst of his pain, he would begin to worship God (Ps. 31). *The soul that leans on the Lord will find perfect peace in the midst of the storm.* (Is. 26:3; Heb. 6:19)

3. **He Honored God's Anointing...Even in Weak Vessels of Clay.** It's shocking to see the extreme honor David gave to Saul, the disgraced king who tried to kill him again and again (2 Sam. 1:17-27). *Those who are able to extract the precious from the vile can speak for God!* (Jer. 15:19)

4. **Even in His Great Success, He Remained Humble Before God.** David never attempted to usurp God's authority or glory. He was genuinely amazed that God had chosen him to be king (2 Sam. 7:18-22). *The mountain of greatness rises from the valley of humility!* (1 Pet. 5:6)

5. **He Was Quick to Repent.** Did David sin? Worse than you, my friend! Read Psalm 32 and 51 and you can see why God's heart was so inclined to him. *One of the greatest qualities a person can possess is to have a tender heart and spirit before the Lord.* (1 Pet. 3:4)

So how can you navigate life when your world falls apart? Learn from David's life and practice these Five Secrets to Greatness. Will God make you a king if you do? No...but the King of Glory will make a place for you in His heart and you'll be rooted and grounded in His love...forever! (Eph. 3:16-21).

What is God's Spirit Saying to Me...
As I Navigate Life According To 2 Samuel

1 KINGS

How to Throw Away Your Heritage... In Four Easy Steps!

Is it possible to walk in God's amazing grace and unimaginable blessings...and then waste it all? Solomon Did. ***If this king, who was wiser than all men, could lose his heritage...what about you and me?***

- What four foolish things did Solomon do that cost him his kingdom?
- What was God's judgment in the matter?
- Remember, your children inherit your legacy...Good or Bad!

How to Throw Away Your Heritage...
In Four Easy Steps!

"Isn't it rich? Are we a pair? Me here at last on the ground; You in mid-air. And where are the clowns? Quick, send in the clowns. Don't bother...They're here." From Broadway to Vegas this stunning ballad was sung by the greatest voices of the 1970's...from Judy Collins to Barbara Streisand to Frank Sinatra. Set to a haunting melody, it's the tragic story of a woman reflecting on the irony and disappointments of life's foolish decisions. Such was the case of the sad story of Solomon. Such is the case with many who are unwittingly throwing away the honor and grace God gave them in exchange for a life of dishonor, disgrace and destroyed heritage!

The First Book of Kings could have been named **"A Parade of Fools!"** Though some kings acted righteously, most were mixed with pagan worship and corruption. Even the great and wise Solomon failed miserably. Look at what happened. *"He had seven hundred wives, princesses, and three hundred concubines, and his wives turned his heart away. For when Solomon was old, his wives turned his heart away after other gods...he went after Ashtoreth the goddess of the Sidonians and after Milcom the detestable idol of the Ammonites. Solomon did what was evil in the sight of the Lord."* (1 Kings 11:3-8). Tragically, this wisest of all kings became foolish. And how did God judge this matter? He ripped the kingdom from Solomon and gave it to men who followed Solomon's example of idolatry (1 Kings 11:9-11). Why did God do this? **To teach us the powerful effect we have on future generations (Ex. 20:5-6).**

And so, dear friend, here are the four ways that Solomon threw his heritage away. If you follow them, it can happen to you too.

1. **Don't Bother to Read God's Word or Heed the Warnings.**
   God's word, His rules for life, and His warnings do NOT have

a statute of limitations nor do they ever expire. God warned the future kings of Israel to not multiply wealth or wives, for they would turn their hearts away from Him (Deut. 17:14-20). Tragically, Solomon violated every one of these warnings (2 Chron. 1:14-17).

2. **Ignore the Wisdom of Your Own Counsel.** Solomon's wisdom was immense! He wrote Ecclesiastes, Song of Solomon and most of Proverbs...3000 proverbs and 1005 songs (1 Kings 4:32). But he violated his own wisdom (Prov. 7:21-27)! *It's amazing how wise our counsel can be for others...but we don't DO what we SAY. Oh that we would heed our own wisdom and live!*

3. **Leave the Gates To Your Heart Wide Open.** From Solomon's own pen, he wrote: *"Above all else, guard your heart, for it is the wellspring of life."* (Prov. 4:23, NIV). He didn't do it! Your heart is the rudder of your emotional life...it can make you do anything! Just as Solomon's heart was turned away from the Lord, so can yours. *A heart left unguarded is open to deception (Jer. 17:9)!*

4. **Disregard Your Conscience.** Your conscience is your basic sense of right and wrong. But if you disregard its warnings long enough, it becomes seared and hardened. As Solomon's heart was slipping away, he justified his actions and ignored the warnings. *Thus his life ended fully engaged in false religions! Your conscience is God's gift to you, my friend...don't ignore its voice!*

Now listen carefully. Twice the Lord visited Solomon and gifted him with unfathomable favor and grace. **But instead of becoming a wise steward of God's gift, he handed the next generation a heritage of foolishness!** Stop and think about this my friend. Remember the Lord's favor and grace in your life. If you realize that any part of this teaching applies to you, it's not too late to change. If for no other reason, do it for your children and grandchildren!

What is God's Spirit Saying to Me...
As I Navigate Life According To 1 Kings

2 KINGS

Life WITHOUT the Anointing
WHERE Is the God of Elijah?

I'm sure you've heard some Christians speak about "The Anointing." Do you think they're a bit extreme or over the top? *You'll be surprised to learn how ESSENTIAL the Anointing really is!*

- What is The Anointing?
- What would life be like if it didn't exist?
- How can you receive God's Anointing in your life?

Life WITHOUT the Anointing
WHERE Is the God of Elijah?

How long can you live without food, water and air? **Three Weeks** without Food...you'll begin to die; **Three Days** without Water...death sets in; **Three Minutes** without air...you're about to lose consciousness and will be dead in three more minutes! So, how long can you "live" without God's anointing? It all depends on how you define "life." If you think it's just eating, drinking and breathing, then the anointing is unimportant to you. But if your life is more than these things (Matt. 6:25-33), it takes on a whole new meaning. If your *"Food"* is doing God's will and accomplishing His work (John 4:32-34); if your *"Drink"* is the water of eternal life (John 4:13-14); if the *"Air"* you breathe is the very Breath of God (Job 33:4; John 20:22), **and if these things define your spiritual life, then you can't LIVE without a constant flow of God's precious anointing!**

This must have been what the young prophet, Elisha, was sensing as he walked alongside of the aged Elijah. During 2 Kings, apostasy was rampant and corruption was a way of life. **In short, most people lived totally without God's anointing!** But not so with Elijah, the old prophet! God's power flowed through him like none other...fearlessly confronting false religions, speaking God's control over nature, calling for miraculous provisions during a famine, even raising the dead! It's no wonder Elisha asked for a double portion of Elijah's spiritual influence (2 Kings 2:9)! It's no wonder that when Elijah was taken up in a whirlwind, Elisha picked up the old prophet's mantle and cried, *"WHERE is the God of Elijah?" (2 Kings 2:14). In other words, "If the God who anointed Elijah and gave him power isn't with me, my life isn't worth living!"*

What then is "The Anointing?" that the Bible speaks about? And what would life be like without it?

1. The Anointing Is God's <u>PRESENCE</u> With You (John 14:16-18). Anointing is far greater than fragrant oil dabbed on your forehead. It's God's Spirit living and working in you...just as He did in Jesus (Acts 10:38; 1 John 2:20). *Life without the anointing of God's Presence means you're on your own without His power! Without God in your life means that you'll run out of "steam" when you need it most (Ex. 33:13-16)!*

2. The Anointing Is God's <u>COMPASSION</u> in You (Luke 4:18-19). Anointing isn't a "Feel-Good" experience...it's "Feeling What God Feels" for people in trouble. And it's not just sympathy. It is divine unction to DO something to help hurting people (Matt. 9:35-38). *Without the anointing of God's Compassion for others, God will NOT have compassion for you (James 2:13-17)!*

3. The Anointing Is the <u>ZEAL</u> of the Lord Filling You (Isa 9:7; John 2:13-17). God's zeal is unlike human emotions. It's the full force of His infinite power thrown into overcoming evil, preserving His truth, advancing His Kingdom and protecting His Church. *Life without <u>God's</u> zeal leaves you trying to champion your own cause without His power (Num. 14:40-43). That's totally disastrous!*

4. The Anointing Is God's <u>GUIDANCE</u> For You (1 John 2:27). The journey of life can lead you down treacherous paths and across barren deserts where many lose their way. God's Spirit is like a divine GPS guiding you to safety (Ps. 143:8-10; Is. 30:21). *Without His anointing, you're blind, hopelessly lost and will certainly fall victim to evil men...or even to your own foolishness!*

5. The Anointing Is God's <u>POWER</u> Working Through You (1 Cor. 2:4-5). Don't confuse talent for anointing! Talent may stir the emotions but the anointing changes lives. God's power

casts out demons, heals the sick, softens hearts, restores sinners and brings eternal life. *Life without God's power flowing through you is shallow, empty and unfulfilled. And that's no life at all!*

So, my friend, do you have God's Anointing in your life? If not, you can have it NOW! It all begins with faith in Jesus *(1 John 5:11-12)*. He's the One who gives the Holy Spirit *(John 15:26)* and anoints you to serve the Lord *(2 Cor. 1:21-22)*. Then, like Elisha, you can live every moment of your life "In His Anointing!"

What is God's Spirit Saying to Me...
As I Navigate Life According To 2 Kings

1 CHRONICLES

My Spiritual DNA
Who Am I Really?

It's amazing how far some people will go to search out their heritage. Many want to discover if their ancestors might be famous. *Most are disappointed...but guess what others discover?*

- What is your DNA and what does it determine?
- Are you trapped by your family DNA and forced to fulfill its destiny?
- What is your "Spiritual" DNA and who are you really?

My Spiritual DNA
Who Am I Really?

"I come from a long line of losers. Half outlaw half boozers. I was born with a shot glass in my hand. I'm part hippie...a little red neck. I'm always a suspect. My blood line made me who I am!" My ears perked up when I heard these swaggering words sung over the radio. Montgomery Gentry's 2008 Country ballad tells the story of a renegade who justifies his corrupt behavior with his family history. Nice try, Mr. Gentry, but for those of us who belong to Christ...YOU'RE WRONG!

Your genealogy is a list of the people who are biological links in the great chain of your life. All your family members are mixed into your DNA (Deoxyribonucleic Acid). It's the genetic blueprint that identifies you as an individual...***chemically that is!*** But your life is more than chemicals! Though your DNA indicates much about your physical identity, it doesn't tell the Whole Story! Biological DNA cannot foretell your Destiny...spiritually or otherwise!

The first 10 chapters of First Chronicles recount a detailed history of the lineage and human events from Adam to David...and even beyond. *(Actually, the content of this book parallels much of 2 Samuel, but was written by a different author.)* If you look carefully at this genealogy, you'd be shocked at how DYSFUNCTIONAL most of these people were. It's the same story for many of us! So...why is there ***"A Long Line of Losers"*** in most families and how should you navigate your life?

1. You Ultimately Came From God...Not Just Biological Parents. Though you bear the physical identity of your fore-parents, God formed you in the spiritual "image and likeness" of His character and nature. ***You were created to be His righteous***

representative on a planet filled with evil and satanic influence (Gen. 1:26-28; Rev. 12:3-4, 7-9).

2. **But Something Went Terribly Wrong!** Instead of confronting evil in the Garden, Adam and Eve fell into its grip! That one-time tragic event had unbelievable consequences. Corruption spread to every living creature on earth...including you and me! *Instead of representing God's righteousness, we selfishly seek our own desires and even participate in evil (Eph. 5:5-12).*

3. **You Can't Ignore the "Tendencies" From Your Natural Bloodline.** Coursing through your veins may be the blood of liars, cheats, carousers, drunkards and murderers (Gal. 5:19-21). If that's not bad enough, weaknesses and diseases are passed through genetic bloodlines. *Forewarned is Forearmed! If you don't guard your mind and body against these things, you'll inherit them!*

4. **But God Redeemed You Back To His Bloodline!** Now this is what that country singer didn't sing about. When you receive Christ as your personal Savior, His blood cleanses you from ALL your sins...past, present and future (Rom. 10:9-10; 1 John 1:7). *Yes, you were part of a "Long Line of Losers"...but in Christ, you are washed, sanctified and justified (1 Cor. 6:9-11)!*

5. **Then Your Spiritual DNA Triumphs Over Your Natural DNA.** Before Christ, the country singer was right...you were stuck with a losing heritage. But because of God's redemptive grace in your life, you have a **Royal Heritage**...You're related to the KING OF KINGS...Jesus! Now you can literally lay aside the old heritage and put on your new Destiny (Eph. 4:22-24). *This is who you REALLY are, my friend...a New Creation in Christ; old things have passed away; behold, all things have become new (2 Cor. 5:17)!*

Now, this is the kind of "Map" you need to have with you at all times ....Scriptures that show you the road to success in God. And with the "Compass" of God's Spirit, you'll always know when you get off of God's course and are headed back to destructive legacies of past generations.

What is God's Spirit Saying to Me...
As I Navigate Life According To 1 Chronicles

2 CHRONICLES

Fatal Counsel
Who You Should NEVER Listen To!

Have you ever been led down a wrong path by someone who gave you bad counsel? Instead of trying to blame them, here's a better idea: ***Learn how to recognize good counsel when you hear it!***

- Two questions you should ask BEFORE you seek counsel.
- What is "Fatal Counsel" and how can you avoid it?
- How can you discern good counsel when you hear it?

Fatal Counsel
Who You Should NEVER Listen To!

What career should I pursue? What management style should I adopt? Who should I marry? When should I buy or sell a house? Where should I go to church? Life is encompassed by the decisions we make. And the quality of our lives depends upon the quality of our decisions. Therefore, ask these questions before you make a decision:

1. Who should I look to for counsel?
2. How do I know if what I'm hearing is good counsel or not?

Why? Because <u>Wrong</u> Counsel is WORSE than <u>NO</u> Counsel at all!

The book of 2 Chronicles is the story of a nation torn in two. Paralleling the events in 1 Kings, it gives another perspective of how Solomon's spiritual failure reached the next generation. His son, Rehoboam, inherited the throne and began his reign the right way...he sought the counsel of the elders who had served his father. But 2 Chron. 10:3-16 tells the rest of the story: ***"He forsook the counsel of the elders which they had given him, and consulted with the young men who grew up with him and served him."*** That fatal error plunged his nation into a full-blown Civil War...***that lasted for 224 years!***

<u>Godly</u> **Counsel** is wise guidance from the Lord that gives you success when faced with difficult life decisions. **<u>Fatal</u> Counsel** is faulty human guidance that leads a naïve person into ultimate failure. **So, who should you listen to for godly counsel?** Consider the following guidelines:

1. **Godly Counselors Will Never Tell You <u>WHAT</u> to Do!** They give PRINCIPLES by which <u>You</u> make your own decisions in life. Principles are fundamental rules or laws of conduct with rewards and consequences. Even God leaves final decisions in your hands (Is. 1:18-20).

2. **Don't Listen To People Who Want To PLEASE You.** That was King Rehoboam's fatal error. The young men he grew up with were subject to his approval or disapproval. They knew what he really wanted to do, so they gave the counsel he wanted to hear. Avoid these people at all costs!

3. **Receive Counsel From Those Who Are SUCCESSFUL or Have Recovered From Setbacks.** It would be foolish to follow the counsel of a person who consistently fails and can't get back on track again. Jesus called them blind guides of the blind...you'll both fall in a pit (Matt. 15:14)!

Next Question: How do you know if what you're hearing is Good Counsel or not?

1. **It Will Never Violate the CHARACTER of God as Revealed in His Word.** If the counsel you receive feeds jealousy, selfishness, arrogance or vengeance in you, REJECT it as fast as you can! Remember, wisdom from God is *"pure, peaceable, gentle, willing to yield, full of mercy and good fruits, without partiality and without hypocrisy"* (James 3:13-18).

2. **Don't Ignore Little INCONSISTENCIES!** If it doesn't make sense...something's wrong! When God is involved in major life-decisions, all the pieces come together in a beautiful mosaic of His plan for your life. Don't disregard Common Sense and Conventional Logic. This doesn't discount His miraculous intervention, but God usually blends the spiritual with the natural (James 2:14-26).

3. **Don't Believe EVERYTHING You Hear...Seek the Lord for Yourself!** Yes, there is safety in the abundance of counselors (Prov. 11:14). But scripture also warns, *"The naive believes everything, but the sensible man considers his steps"* (Prov. 14:15). Weigh counsel from others with the warnings the Lord

has placed in your heart. Remember, <u>You</u> are responsible for your life, not a counselor!

So, my friend, that's the "Map" of 2 Chronicles. When you follow it, you'll avoid the side-roads and dead-end streets of wrong counsel. Now, be attentive to the "Compass" of God's Spirit. With these two "Navigational" Instruments, you'll be able to navigate life successfully.

What is God's Spirit Saying to Me...
As I Navigate Life According To 2 Chronicles

EZRA

God's Remnant
Appalled at the Slow Cook of the Church!

Every now and then you'll meet a person of rare character. They refuse to cave-in to pressures that tempt them to "sell-out" their faith. ***They're called God's Remnant. Are <u>You</u> one of them?***

- The "Slow Cook"...What is it and how does it happen?
- Who is God's Remnant and what do they do?
- Five ways to know if you're getting "Cooked" or if you're part of God's Remnant.

God's Remnant
Appalled at the Slow Cook of the Church!

"If you throw a frog in boiling water, he'll quickly jump out. But if you put him in a pan of cold water and ever so slowly raise the temperature, **the gradual warming will make the frog doze happily until he gets cooked to death...without ever waking up!"** Do you think this is just an old folk story? Well, it really happened in Ezra's day. And it's happening again today...in God's Church!

Ezra lived in the time when Israel was returning from exile in Babylon. During those seventy years of God's Judgment, the corrupt generation that had **mixed their faith with world religions** died off and a new generation returned to start their lives over again with God. **But 80 years later, corruption set in again!** When Ezra stepped onto the scene, he discovered that even the **Priests** and **Levites** had married pagan women and had re-engaged in pagan worship! And what's wrong with that you ask? Their children and everyone they influence would believe that it's acceptable to stray from the one true God. When Ezra saw this, he sat down **APPALLED**, tore his clothes and cried out to God (Ezra 9:1-8)!

God's Remnant is His "Faithful Few" who tenaciously hold to God's standards when others fall away. They have been rescued and cleansed from sin and are commissioned as God's righteous witnesses in a corrupt world full of mixture. When they see the *"Slow Cook of the Frog,"* they warn people who don't perceive the danger! So, the Big Question is this: Are you the "Frog" or the "Remnant?" Here's how you can know:

1. If You're **APATHETIC** About the Moral Decay in America...*You're Getting Cooked!* Think back when you were a child. Was there confusion between Right and Wrong? Was it acceptable to live together and have children without

marriage? Were four-letter words common in movies? Was gender confusion applauded? Remember Is. 5:20! *Apathy is the first sign of being Cooked!*

2. If You Believe GOD'S WORD Is Anything the Preacher Says...*You're Getting Cooked!* God's Remnant will read and study the Bible for themselves. Like the Bereans, you must *"search the scriptures daily to find out whether these things are so" (Acts 17:11)*. *If what you're hearing from the pulpit doesn't line up with the "whole counsel" of God's word (from Genesis to Revelation), don't buy into it! (Gal. 1:6-9)*

3. If You're Not Appalled at the Religious MIXTURE in God's Church...*You're Getting Cooked!* There is a demonic deception creeping into today's churches. It's an eclectic belief system that tries to convince you that all faiths are equally true and that it doesn't matter what you believe. *That's called "Mixture," my friend! It's slow-acting poison!* (2 Cor. 6:14-17; 1 John 4:1-3)

4. If You're Not PRACTICING What You Preach...*You're Getting Cooked!* Ezra was a classic example of God's Righteous Remnant in the earth. *"He set his heart to **Study** the law of the Lord and to **Practice** it, and to **Teach** His statutes and ordinances in Israel"* (Ezra 7:10). *Thinking that you're an exception to God's standards is a sure sign of being Cooked!*

5. If You're COMPROMISING Your Christian Beliefs to Keep Friends or Places of Favor...*You're Getting Cooked!* It's amazing how subtle deception is. It'll make you sit under false teaching just to keep from losing your title or a place of influence. Friends and ministry positions are important, but they can't get you to heaven! *God's Remnant maintains friendships, but not if it could cost them their souls! They never sell-out for places of honor* (Matt. 16:24-26).

So, how can you navigate your Destiny from the Book of Ezra? Ask God to help you become His Remnant...right where you live. **Take heed to these warnings and you'll never end up like the "Frog!"**

What is God's Spirit Saying to Me...
As I Navigate Life According To Ezra

NEHEMIAH

Rebuilding Your Spiritual Life...
After it Falls Apart!

Betrayal of trust is devastating! But when it happens in God's Church, it can shake the very foundations of your faith. Some people NEVER get over it. *So what can you do when the "Unthinkable" happens?*

- What does the book of Nehemiah have to do with all of this?

- Two things to remember when the unthinkable happens.

- Four things you must do if you're going to rebuild the spiritual foundation of your faith.

Rebuilding Your Spiritual Life... After it Falls Apart!

There it was...plastered on the front page of the morning paper; the lead story of the evening news; and the reason your phone was ringing off the hook. Another pastor had fallen from grace to disgrace! But this time it was different. *This time the scandalous story was about <u>YOUR</u> church and <u>YOUR</u> pastor!*

In the pale moonlit night, a rider secretly made his way to the ruins of what "used to be." Even in the shadows of darkness, the horror that had come upon his beloved city of Jerusalem was overwhelming. The mighty walls of Zion lay in rubble with its gates burned out. *The once great and honored city called Jerusalem was laying in desolation...a haunting reminder of the unbelievable cost of forsaking the Lord.* (Neh. 2:12-15)

What do these two stories have in common? They represent centers of spiritual life for God's people...fortresses of faith and towers of light. They're supposed to be unshakable refuges where the weary are refreshed, sinners are cleansed and the child of God is taught the way of righteousness. But when these "Cities of God" collapse in ruin, it leaves believers confused, groping for answers and reeling in disbelief. **When the "Unthinkable" happens, remember these two things:**

1. **Neither Jerusalem Nor the Church Is God!** Idolatry is placing your spiritual confidence in inanimate objects or people or institutions! Buildings deteriorate and so do people! *But those who set their hearts on God will never be moved...regardless of what or who fails* (Is. 26:3-4; Heb. 12:28).

2. **God's Church Is BIGGER Than Your Little World.** The "Church" you can <u>SEE</u> is the community of believers organized with human authorities. Unfortunately they have the

same ability to fail as you do! But there's also the "Church" you CANNOT SEE...it exists in the realm of faith. It's comprised of ALL believers in the Lord Jesus (past, present and future) who are recipients of His saving grace. *Those who trust in Jesus and confess their sins are cleansed and made righteous in Him.*

So, how can you navigate your life when the spiritual trust you've placed in your church and pastor falls apart? **Do what Nehemiah did. Rebuild!** This is how he did it and this is how you can too:

1. **Seek Forgiveness and Pray (Neh. 1:3-7).** We're all disappointed by human failure. But if your faith in God has been shaken, your priorities are wrong! Jesus is THE role model...not a person or a church (Heb. 12:1-2). *Pray for those who failed...they're in more trouble than you are!*

2. **Survey the Ruins (Neh. 2:12-18; 1:7-9).** Even though it's painful, look closely at the devastation and learn what caused it to happen. You, my friend, are not immune to sin either. *Examine your ways carefully knowing this could happen to you too (Gal. 6:1-9)!*

3. **Get a Plan and Rebuild Your Spiritual Foundation (Neh. 3).** Nehemiah didn't do this alone...and neither can you. Don't fall into the trap of giving up on God or His Church. Seek counsel from mature believers who have weathered life's storms. Then begin rebuilding the foundation of your faith on THE SOLID ROCK. That foundation is the Lord Jesus Christ...not fallible people or institutions (1 Cor. 3:11).

4. **Recognize and Stop the Schemes of the Enemy (Neh. 4).** When Satan sees that you're determined to rebuild your spiritual life, he'll do anything and everything to stop you. Guard yourself and make up your mind you're going to rebuild your life...no matter what (Neh. 6:1-4; Eph. 6:11-17)!

What is God's Spirit Saying to Me...
As I Navigate Life According To Nehemiah

ESTHER

Swimming With the Sharks
Fish Food or a Fish Fry!

"Swimming with the Sharks"...It's one thing to casually use that phrase, but it's a whole different matter if you've been thrown in a REAL Shark-Pool! *It's either Eat or be Eaten!*

- What was Esther's Shark-Pool and how did God help her?
- What kind of "Shark" is the worst of all?
- What can you do when you see Fins circling around you?

Swimming With the Sharks
Fish Food or a Fish Fry!

Okay, so who's crazy enough to "Swim with the Sharks?" Only daredevils, fools or the poor fellow whose boat sank and he saw fins circling him. Sharks are fearsome predators in water; but on land, the two-legged ones are just as vicious! Harvey Mackay wrote about two-legged sharks in his 1988 business strategy book. If you've ever visited Las Vegas, you might have been eaten alive by one of them at the gaming tables. *But the kind Esther found herself swimming with was worst of all! It was an ancient spirit embedded in a world system of government. Its favorite pastime was devouring God's people!*

The book of Esther is the story of a young Jewish girl, orphaned and adopted by her older cousin, Mordecai. They were captives in Susa, the royal city of Persia. That in itself was like living in a shark-pool. But what happened next was an incredible drama of God's Providence. **Haman, a high official under the king of Persia, was a descendent of Amalek...grandson of Esau who sought to kill his brother, Jacob (Gen. 27:41).** Haman, like his ancestors, was consumed with pride, power and prejudice. He despised the Jews and wanted them exterminated! **But God providentially positioned Esther into a place of extreme favor with the king**...so much so that he loved her and she became his queen (Esth. 2). From that place of favor, Esther uncovered Haman's plot and the king hanged him on the same gallows he intended for Mordecai (Esth. 7)! With his death, the ancient spirit that inhabited Haman no longer had a vessel to work through. *Thus the "shark" that thought the Jews would be "Fish Food" was invited to his own "Fish Fry!"*

Do you feel like you've been thrown into a shark-pool? **It may be treacherous co-workers, cold-blooded creditors or a life-threatening health crisis.** If you think you're being set up as Fish Food, would you want God do for you what He did for Esther? Here's how to navigate your Destiny in a shark-pool:

1. **Seek Godly Counsel and Consider Your Options.** Esther's counselor was her adopted spiritual father, Mordecai. But he didn't sugarcoat his counsel...it was either eat or be eaten! He reminded her of God's Providential hand...she had come to the Kingdom for that very purpose (Esth. 4:13-14). *If you meet the criteria of Rom. 8:28, God can turn your predicament into a Providential Miracle.*

2. **Ask God to Show You What's Really Going On.** Haman's actions in Esth. 3:1-6 were more than arrogance; they were the presence of evil! It was the same evil that had overcome his forefather, Esau (Heb. 12:15-17). Just as evil was embedded in the Persian hierarchy, it can be the active agent working to destroy you. *Remember, spirits will never repent...they must be dealt with by God!*

3. **Know Who You Are and the Favor God Has Given You.** You may not be a queen with the favor of a king...but look at who you really are. You are betrothed to the <u>KING of Glory</u> (Hos. 2:19-20)! You are the "Beloved of the Lord" with access to <u>THE King's Heart</u> (2 Thess. 2:13)! *Call upon Him when you're in trouble and He will surely come to your rescue (Ps. 46:1; Heb. 4:16).*

4. **Consecrate Yourself, Courageously Step Into Your Destiny and Trust God.** Just as Queen Esther consecrated herself to the Lord in Esth. 4:16, so should you when your livelihood or life is at risk. *Why? Unless you're close to God, you really will be Fish Food!* Then read again the three points above. If you really believe them, don't back away regardless of who or what opposes you. Trust the Lord, my friend. *Only God Can Reverse Evil and Turn It Into Good!*

Here's one final thing to consider: What if this dilemma is <u>NOT</u> just about you? The Lord may have set you in a strategic place (like Esther) to bring deliverance to many! That totally changes the dynamics...*from personal survival to a divine assignment of ministry to help the helpless.*

What is God's Spirit Saying to Me...
As I Navigate Life According To Esther

JOB

When Tragedy Strikes
Finding Destiny Out of Disaster

Tornados, Floods and Tsunamis have destroyed lives ever since sin entered the world. But when it happens to YOUR friends or to YOU, it takes on new meaning. *How then shall you live when tragedy strikes?*

- Why do bad things happen to good people and why does God allow it?
- What should you do when tragedy strikes your community?
- How can Destiny be found out of the very thing that threatens to destroy it?

When Tragedy Strikes
Finding Destiny Out of Disaster

In disbelief we listen to breaking news stories of tornados and floods that sweep away innocent people to their deaths. In horror we watch human suffering televised in our community and around the world. And we hold our loved-ones even closer to us. Tragedy is all around us indiscriminately striking saints and sinners alike. **If it befalls your friends, what can you do or say? If you become its victim, will it change how you view God? Is it possible that you can find Destiny out of the very thing that threatens to destroy it?** Maybe we can find some answers from the life of Job...a man who lost everything!

Job was a desert prince, extremely wealthy and prominent in his community. Oh yes, one more thing...***Job was "blameless and upright, and one who feared God and shunned evil"*** (Job 1:1). Then out of "nowhere" he was violently hit with the unthinkable. All of his livestock were stolen, his servants were slaughtered and a thunderstorm killed all ten of his children—ALL IN ONE DAY (Job 1:13-19)! And if that wasn't enough, he was stricken with an incurable disease! Then to add insult to injury, his wife turned against him and told him he might just as well *"Curse God and die!"* (Job 2:7-9).

Out of this horror story, two questions arise...both philosophical and theological in nature: **1) - Why do bad things happen to good people and why does God allow this? 2) - Will a man who claims to be righteous reject God and discard his faith in the face of physical disaster and total loss?** How then shall we navigate life from the principles found in the book of Job?

1. **Bad Things Happen Because We Live in a Fallen World. It's <u>NEVER</u> Because of God!** The events that transpired between God and Satan are intriguing (Job 1:6-12; 2:1-7). But don't think you've been reduced to a human "bargaining chip" that

God uses against Satan. The problem was Adam's failure to do what God commanded and to take dominion over Satan and his deception (Gen. 1:28; 3:11-13). *Because Adam didn't stop evil in the Garden, it was released on the world with suffering, pain and premature death (Gen. 3:17-19).*

2. **Don't Be Like Job's "Friends."** Well-meaning friends can be worse than enemies! Instead of praying for Job or even trying to help him, they folded their arms and declared his suffering was God's judgment upon his life! Neither they nor Job had a clue of what was really happening. *And so it is with us if we try to judge people when tragedy strikes them (Luke 13:1-5)!*

3. **Get a New Attitude....*About God and People!*** Job and his friends got a major attitude adjustment when God stepped on the scene (Job 38-42). All vain explanations of human suffering were blown away when God spoke out of a massive tornado totally beyond their control. And what did God tell them to do? *Seek forgiveness and pray for one another...then I'll restore you!* When Job did this, God restored all that Job had lost (Job 42:1-6, 10).

4. **Can Anything Good Come Out of Tragedy?** *Your Destiny Can!* As destructive as disaster is, God can use it to REFINE your faith and purpose in life (1 Pet. 1:6-7; James 1:2-4, 12)! Like the refining process for precious metals, suffering can strip away insignificant and useless ways of living. In the face of losing everything, your eternal relationship with God becomes paramount (Eccles. 12:6-7, 13-14). Once Job learned this, God restored everything back to him...twice as much along with a better Destiny (Job 42:10-17)! *Your Destiny is more than your possessions or career...it's what you do for God and for others throughout your life!*

How then shall you live when tragedy strikes? Live with *__Compassion__* for those who suffer. This means *__Praying__* for the helpless AND *__Being__*

There for them in their time of need. Live with ***Gratitude*** for the days the Lord has given you. Live with ***Renewed Purpose*** to fulfill the Destiny to which God has called you. Live with ***Eternal Trust*** in God...regardless of what happens to you or in the world around you!

What is God's Spirit Saying to Me...
As I Navigate Life According To Job

PSALMS

Unhappy? Angry? Afraid? How Honest Can You Be With God?

Ever feel like you have to tip-toe around sensitive issues when talking with God? Afraid to tell Him how you REALLY feel about...well, you know who or you know what? *If so, then you'll be shocked to read what the Psalmists wrote!*

- How honest can I get with God?
- Do righteous people really feel what I'm feeling?
- How can I navigate my Destiny when I come to the end of my rope?

Unhappy? Angry? Afraid?
How Honest Can You Be With God?

"Take this job and_____! I ain't workin' here no more!" Ever felt like singing that old 1977 outlaw-country song? If you're human, you probably have. Along the journey of your Destiny, you're going to have good days, bad days and days when you just want to throw in the towel (or throw it at somebody). The amazing thing about God is that He knows how fragile our human condition is. He knows what we're feeling even before we express it! He knows our fallen natures can at times get the best of us. In fact, the worst thing you can do is try to suppress your feelings to God...they just might putrefy and erupt into violence! **This means you can be HONEST with God about how you feel...*as long as you follow the pattern of the Psalms.***

The Psalms portray God's people, their struggles, sins, sorrows, joys, failures and victories. They are expressions of the heart and mind of man toward God and while trying to live righteously. **You may not know it, but there's a Psalm for almost every season in your life:**

1. Are you <u>Afraid</u> and need <u>Reassurance</u> of God's protection?— *Read Psalms 27, 56, 91, 140-143.*

2. Are you <u>Angry</u> at someone who hurt you? *Read Psalms 35, 58, 69, 109.* (These are called the Imprecatory Psalms.)

3. Are you <u>Sorrowful</u> for your own sinfulness? *Read Psalms 32, 51.* (These are called the Penitential Psalms.)

4. Are you <u>Thankful</u> for God's rich blessings in your life? *Read Psalms 135-136, 138-139.*

5. Do you just feel like <u>Praising</u> the Lord? *Read Psalms 113-118 & 146-150.* (These are called the Hallel Psalms.)

6. Would you like to see <u>Jesus</u> in the Psalms? ***Read Psalms 2, 8, 16, 22, 45, 72, 89, 110, 118, 132.*** (These are the Messianic Psalms written 1000 years before Christ.)

7. Do you want to be reminded of God's <u>Sovereignty</u>? ***Read Psalms 98, 115, 145, 146.***

8. Would you like to see the <u>Hand of God</u> in human history? ***Read Psalms 105, 106.***

9. Looking for something to read before going to church? ***Read Psalms 120-134.*** (These are the Songs of Ascent.)

So, how can you navigate your Destiny when you come to the end of your rope and are frustrated beyond measure? Follow the pattern of the Psalmists:

1. **Be Honest With God.** The psalmists didn't suppress their love for God or their frustrations in life. If you've been hurt by someone close to you, tell God how you feel. If you're haunted by your past, confide in the Lord. If you're afraid, tell Him what scares you the most. If you really love God, don't hold back! ***Your open honesty draws the Lord's heart near to you.***

2. **Be Honest...But Never Blame God for Bad Things That Happen.** The psalmists knew that God is never the cause of human problems...He's the solution! They were quick to confess their sins, draw near to God and call upon His grace, mercy and protective power. ***When evil approaches your door, run quickly to His throne and seek refuge in His mighty arms.***

3. **Be Honest, But in the End Embrace God's Goodness by Rehearsing Past Victories.** Whenever the psalmists were depressed or worried, they would gain strength and courage by

remembering the goodness of the Lord. When trouble surrounds you and you don't know which way to turn, think back to the last time He kept you from destruction...even when you weren't aware that He was there. *Trust God...He's the same, yesterday, today and forever!*

4. **Be Honest, But Always Temper Your Actions With The Character of Christ.** Sure, you feel hurt and angry and desire revenge. The psalmists felt the same way. It's okay to express these feelings to the Lord...just like they did. He's big enough to handle them. *But when it comes to your actions, follow Jesus' teachings in Matt. 5-7. The way of Christ never returns evil for evil.*

What is God's Spirit Saying to Me...
As I Navigate Life According To Psalms

PROVERBS

God's Handbook of Common Sense Wisdom for Dummies!

Do you know people who continually fall in the same ditch over and over again? Wonder why they don't wise up? Maybe they need this teaching. ***Maybe we could ALL use a good dose of this!***

- What's "Common Sense" and why do we need it?
- Want to see how practical being spiritual can really be?
- Five ways to use the book of Proverbs and stay out of trouble.

God's Handbook of Common Sense Wisdom for Dummies!

"Common Sense" is a misnomer...it's not very common! Created in God's image, we are supposed to exercise sound judgment based on simple perceptions of situations. But unfortunately people have a tendency to "leap before they look," to develop self-defeating habits and to naively walk into obvious traps set by predators. One reason why Common Sense isn't very common is because our basic Life-Standards have been diluted or totally discarded. *The end result is that people live in the "Gray Areas" of life with no contrast between right and wrong!*

Three thousand years before Dan Gookin wrote his first *"For Dummies"* book, God published HIS BOOK for people who have fatal attractions to do dumb things! It's called the book of Proverbs. It's a compilation of divinely inspired wise sayings that makes spirituality very practical. The term "proverb" comes from a root word which means to rule or take dominion. **In other words, if you read this book, you'll be able to RULE your life with WISDOM!** Here are some examples of God's Handbook of Common Sense and how it can keep you out of trouble...**IF** you actually USE His Wisdom in your life. Remember, there's a Proverb for Every "<u>STUPID</u>" Season in Life!

1. Do you believe that good decisions can be made if you <u>Follow Your Heart</u>? *Read Prov. 28:26.*

2. Are you <u>Offended</u>? Want to give people the <u>Silent Treatment</u>? *Read Prov. 18:1; 19:11; 25:21-22.*

3. Are you considering <u>Co-signing</u> to help a friend buy a new car? *Read Prov. 22:26-27.*

4. Are you tempted to chase after money and **"Get Rich Quick" Schemes**? *Read Prov. 23:4-5.*

5. Do you like to **Jump in the Middle** of other people's arguments? *Read Prov. 26:17.*

6. Do you **Hate** to be **Disciplined** or **Corrected**? *Read Prov. 12:1; 15:10.*

7. Think you can **"Mess Around"** with another person's wife or husband and not get caught? *Read Prov. 6:20-35.*

So, how can you use "God's Handbook of Common Sense" to navigate your life? Here's a good step-by-step suggestion to make life easier and a lot less painful:

1. **A Proverb a Day Keeps Stupidity Away!** Set a pattern of reading one chapter in Proverbs each day. Since there are 31 chapters, you can read the chapter that relates to each day of the month.

2. **Choose Your Favorite "Zingers."** A zinger is something that makes you say "Oh My...that is **Sooo** true!" Underline and memorize favorite proverbs that will keep you out of trouble in the future.

3. **Application! Application! Application!** Wisdom without application is like getting a prescription from your doctor and never taking it. If you don't use the wisdom God gives you, it's useless.

4. **Show Others How Smart You Are.** Find opportunities to share the wisdom you've learned with other people. They'll be amazed at how smart you got in such a short period of time!

5. **Multiply Your Wisdom.** God's wisdom is not just in Proverbs; it's everywhere in the Bible. As you read, ask God for His wisdom. He wants you to have it even more than you do (James 1:5)!

What is God's Spirit Saying to Me...
As I Navigate Life According To Proverbs

ECCLESIASTES

LIFE
The ULTIMATE Reality Show!

Pastors have a unique assignment. God trusts us to minister to people during difficult challenges and struggles in their lives. ***We don't deny reality, but we point them to a greater reality...God!***

- What does the book of Ecclesiastes have to do with modern TV shows?

- Was Solomon just an old cynic...or was he speaking to a greater reality than the vanities of life?

- How can the struggles of life be turned into hope and confidence?

LIFE
The ULTIMATE Reality Show!

They exploded into insane popularity in the late 1990's...unscripted dramatic televised situations featuring ordinary people instead of professional actors. They call it "REALITY TV." Shows like "Survivor," "Fear Factor," "The Biggest Loser," "Super Nanny" and "The Bachelor" grab people's attentions and glue them to their TV sets. Basically, it's a *"sit in your armchair with a bag of chips"* event watching OTHER people suffer from bad decisions and foolish actions. (I suppose it makes people feel better about their own problems.) **Newsflash...you don't have to tune in to network TV to get a big dose of reality. You're IN your own Ultimate Reality Show...it's called LIFE and you're playing the lead role!**

Ecclesiastes is one of the most startling "Reality" books in the Bible. It's written by Solomon, who calls himself "The Preacher." *(That's what the word "Ecclesiastes" means.)* Some call Solomon an old cynic and others call him a realist. But one thing is for sure, he cuts right to the chase and reveals humanity in its most raw and vulnerable form. That's why he begins his book like this: **"Vanity of vanities. All is vanity!"** Solomon had acquired more wealth and material possessions and had enjoyed more pleasure than any human being on earth. In other words... **"I've been there, done that, got the T-shirt...Now What? Is there anything that can bring lasting purpose in my life besides what I've already done?"**

If you've lived a long time and seen too much of "Real Life," like Solomon did, you may have a tendency to agree with his caustic prose. **But God is a greater than life's disappointments!** Tucked away in this "painfully honest" book are insights into how you should navigate life. Here are a few:

1. Don't Try To Fill Your Life With "<u>STUFF</u>!" Solomon, who had EVERYTHING, discovered that possessions, fleshly pleasures and even natural wisdom are all VANITY (Eccles. 1-2). *Why? Because the more you have...the more you want! (Eccles. 5:10-11).*

2. True <u>FULFILLMENT</u> Can Never Be Found Apart From God. As I'm sure you've heard before, there is a "God-shaped" void in every human heart. Nothing can fill that void except the presence of the Eternal and Living God who created you. *Try as you may, you'll never be satisfied apart from the Savior's love and approval in your life. (Eccles. 2:25; 3:11-14).*

3. <u>ACCOUNTABILITY</u> To Your Creator Brings Meaning To Life. Human beings are strange creatures. We need boundaries, yet we resist them. Knowing how far we can go and can't go actually brings security. But we try to throw off the very thing that keeps us right with God. *The Reality that one day you'll have to stand before the Lord to give an answer for how you've lived creates "Value-Living"...Living with Godly Purpose. (Eccles. 3:17; 12:13-14).*

4. Don't Let <u>OLD AGE</u> Stop You From Honoring the Lord. *He's the Same as When You Were Young!* Sure, the older we get, the more difficult life becomes. Our bodies really do wear down with age. But don't let the problems of aging make you forget the Lord. Honor Him as when you were young. Serve God all the days of your life and trust in Jesus. *Then when life's road comes to an end, He'll reward you in heaven (Eccles. 12:1-7).*

Yes, my friend, Life is the Ultimate Reality Show. Remember, it's life's real <u>STRUGGLES</u> that make Reality Shows so intriguing! If there were no ups and downs, no twists and turns, and no risk of failure in the lives of REAL people, no one would ever watch those shows. If you navigate your life according to the "Map" of Ecclesiastes, you'll live your life with confidence knowing that you're pleasing the Lord. If you follow the "Compass" of God's Spirit, you'll successfully arrive at your Destiny...regardless of how difficult life becomes.

What is God's Spirit Saying to Me...
As I Navigate Life According To Ecclesiastes

SONG OF SOLOMON

Up Close and Personal... With God!

"The 5 Love Languages" is a powerful book on how to express and interpret love in marriage. ***You'll be shocked to read God's "Love Language" book (written in human terms)! It's called "Song of Solomon."***

- Song of Solomon. It's provocative, unashamed and open in its expressions of intimacy. Can you handle it?
- Why some people totally miss its true meaning.
- You'll NEVER achieve your destiny unless you get *"Up Close and Personal"* with God!

Up Close and Personal... With God!

What Does God Look Like? Is He Austere? Is He a towering old man with long gray hair and a beard with flowing white robes and sandals? Maybe He's leaning to the side pointing a "shame on you" finger in your face? **How Would You Approach Him...Even If You Could?** Crawling and begging for mercy? Or maybe you'd just cringe in a fetal position hoping He wouldn't see you? **What Would He Say To You?** Would it be... *"Who are you? What are you doing in My Presence? Go away; you have too much sin in your life!"* I'm sure you don't see God like that...but some people do! **Even fewer would dare to think that Solomon's Song portrays a "Passionate Love Relationship" between God and His people!**

With such open and explicit sensual language, some feel this book is inappropriate for "HOLY" Scripture. Others dismiss its theological value believing it's just a Jewish poem extolling free communication of human love. In truth, it reveals the private love-language between two lovers...King Solomon and a Shulammite maiden. However, for those of us who are Christians, this short book is a great portrait of the intimate love between Christ and His Church. *The King represents Jesus and the Bride represents His Church...those who embrace Jesus as their Lord, Savior and King.*

"Okay," you might say, *"If I accept your interpretation of Song of Solomon, how does it help me in everyday life? Even if I thought I could get 'Up Close and Personal' with God, how can I navigate my life with this book? Am I supposed to whisper 'Sweet Nothings' to a God I can't see?"* Consider this:

1. What if God is <u>DIFFERENT</u> Than What You Think? And He is! Though God is the awesome Creator of the universe, He is very **PERSONAL** and very **APPROACHABLE**. In fact,

He seeks for <u>you</u> knowing that you cannot find Him without His help (Jer. 29:11-13; Ezek. 34:16). God knows your name; *He loves you and will come to you when you call upon Him (Is. 43:1-2).*

2. **What if God Sees <u>YOU</u> Differently Than You Think?** According to Solomon's words to his beloved, God desires to be "Up Close and Personal" with you! He sees you as "Beautiful" even though you feel insecure in His presence (Song 1:5, 15; 4:1). Where does your "Beauty" come from? *Is it not from the Holy Spirit, who is preparing you to be Christ's Bride? (Ps. 45:11-14; Rev. 21:2).*

3. **What if God Created Human Love and Devotion to Help Us Understand <u>SPIRITUAL INTIMACY</u> with Him?** Paul wrote about this amazing spiritual relationship in Eph. 5:23-32. More perfect than a human husband/wife union, Christ's love is so deep and personal that He actually gave His life for you. *In fact, His love is what draws you to Himself (1 John 4:16, 19).*

4. **The Closer You Get to God, the More You Learn About Him...and Yourself!** Spiritual Intimacy means that your life is intermingled with the life of God. In the extreme closeness of your "moment" with God, you can share your innermost thoughts with Him and then He shares His thoughts with you (Ps. 139:17)! You can tell Him your concerns...and then His concerns become yours! Why? *Because you are His Bride (Rev. 21:9)!*

5. **During Your Intimate Times With The Lord, He Navigates Your Life.** Because God created you, He knows what's best for you. (He really does!) He reveals his kind intentions for you and then directs (navigates) your life to achieve greatness in Him (Is. 48:17 NIV). *That's why you cannot discover or achieve your divine Destiny without this <u>very</u> personal relationship with Jesus.*

Listen closely, my friend. There's a big difference between loving God and being "In Love" with Him. It's good to study theology and doctrine. But don't forget to LOVE Jesus. He's the Lover of your soul!

What is God's Spirit Saying to Me...
As I Navigate Life According To Song of Solomon

ISAIAH

Got Prophecy?
Can't Reach Your Destiny Without It!

Does God still speak to people today? Most Christians agree that He speaks through His word, the Bible. *But if you think that's the ONLY way God can speak to you, you're missing a real blessing!*

- Who are prophets and what is prophecy?
- Can the prophet Isaiah, who lived nearly 2,800 years ago, help you to navigate your life today?
- Do prophets still exist today...or have they ceased to function in the church?

Got Prophecy?
Can't Reach Your Destiny Without It!

Some people say they don't exist anymore. Others think they're religious charlatans who prey on the naïve. But for those of us who have received genuine prophetic words from true prophets, our lives will never be the same! **True prophets of God see the end from the beginning.** They warn people of life's storms before they form and they speak of God's restoration while lives are still reeling in destruction. They speak of God's kind intentions for your life, yet they always leave final decisions in your hands. Such was the prophet Isaiah who was the voice of God to the nations!

The book of Isaiah is the beginning of the section in the Bible called "The Prophets." God raised up these men to speak to nations who were headed in the wrong direction...even into utter destruction! *Their Mission: Bring people to an encounter with God with an opportunity for repentance.* But their message wasn't always "gloom, doom and judgment." They spoke of God's **LOVE** toward people; His **GRACE** that gave them a way out of their mess; and promises of glorious **RESTORATION**...if they would only listen. *They spoke of Messiah...the One who would rescue people from self-destructing sin!*

God knows **EVERYTHING** about you...and He loves you anyway! Regardless of the "mess" that may be in your life or in the lives of those you love, God has a solution...if only you will listen! How then does the book of Isaiah help you to navigate the Destiny of your life? *<u>Listen to what the prophet Isaiah is saying to you...even now!</u>*

1. God Wants To "Reason" With You (Is. 1:18-20). God doesn't just sit on some big throne in heaven throwing out orders and issuing judgments. He wants to help you "think things through." Like a good friend, God appeals to your sense of logic about your situation. *Wouldn't it be better to listen to*

God than to die? God wants to heal you...not judge you! (Ezek. 33:11).

2. Beware of "Substitutes" in Your Life (Is. 5:20). The fallen world we live in is filled with alternatives to what God knows is best for you (Is. 48:17 NIV). If you listen to their voices, they'll make you think that it's okay to live any way you want. They'll try to convince you that evil is good and good is evil. *If you walk in their paths, your Destiny with God will be "History!"*

3. Whenever You're In Trouble...God Will Always Be There For You (Is. 25:4). When you make the Lord your God and trust in His strength, He reaches out to you with great compassion. He reverses evil and dispels plans of the ruthless that are against you. He defends you when you're helpless and protects you from calamity. *That's how much God really loves and cares for you!*

4. True Prophecy Is God's Providential Hand Leading You to Your Destiny (Is. 30:21; 42:16). When you need it the most, God steps into your life with a life-giving prophetic word from His heart. Remember what prophecy does...it strengthens, encourages and comforts you (1 Cor. 14:3). *Now you understand why I said, "You can't reach your Destiny without God's Prophetic Words over your life"*

Finally, What About <u>Modern Day Prophets</u>...Do They Really Exist? There are some who try to convince people that Apostles and Prophets ceased to exist after the early church. Oh Really? Show me one scripture that says that! *And don't try to use 1 Cor. 13:8-10 as your proof text.* Paul wrote those words to the Corinthian church that prided themselves in spiritual gifts, but neglected love! He never intended it to mean that prophecy or knowledge should stop in the church. *It's too late to convince me that Prophets don't exist. I KNOW THEM personally! They've spoken into my life and the lives of my family! Their prophetic words encourage others in keeping with*

*1 Cor. 14:3 and they never violate the character of God as revealed in Scripture. Has God used prophecy to confirm my Destiny? Do I believe God still sets Prophets in the church today? **ABSOLUTELY YES!*** Open your heart to the Lord, my friend, and do not despise Prophecy or His Prophets. (1 Thess. 5:20).

What is God's Spirit Saying to Me...
As I Navigate Life According To Isaiah

JEREMIAH

Stepping Into the Heart of God
Could You Handle It?

Want to get close to God? How close do you want to get...close enough to sense His thoughts and feel what He feels? *If God really opened His heart to you, are you sure you could handle it?*

- What does God think about? Jeremiah found out!
- If God let you step into His heart, what would happen to you?
- Can God trust you with what He feels?

Stepping Into the Heart of God Could You Handle It?

What Does God think about? What are the burdens of His heart? Do His thoughts stir His emotions? For most people, these questions never cross their minds. Tragically, the human race is so self-absorbed in their own problems, personal desires and short-term frustrations that they don't even think about how God feels. **What if, just for a fleeting moment, God let you step into His heart to sense what He's feeling?** *"But would God ever do that?"* you may ask. Absolutely! He did it in 66 books. It's called the Bible. **And what happened when Jeremiah stepped into God's heart? He couldn't stop crying!**

Jeremiah is called the "Weeping Prophet." His ministry was during the same turbulent times in Israel as when Isaiah lived...except things were about **100 years** worse! The northern kingdom of Israel had become reprobate beyond remedy. So much so that God had to wipe out that entire region. The southern kingdom ignored every warning God gave and was going down the same path of destruction. In short...the actions of God's people "Broke" His Heart! And they still do today! So, my friend, if YOU stepped into God's Heart with Jeremiah, here's what would happen to you:

1. You'd Realize How Much God LOVES You...*Even After You've Failed Him (Jer. 31:3)!* Jeremiah recorded Israel's blatant sins that forced God's hand of judgment. But he also foresaw God's desire to restore them after their judgment. Listen to how God reaches out to you: *"I have loved you with an everlasting love; therefore I have drawn you with lovingkindness."*

2. You'd See God's Amazing DESTINY for Your Life...*Even Though You Don't Deserve It (Jer. 29:10-14).* Jeremiah was so close to God that he could actually pick up on His thoughts

and plans for Israel. Though God had to severely discipline them, their Destiny was still intact. *Regardless of how far you've strayed, when you return to God with a humble heart, He'll restore you to your Destiny in Him!*

3. You'd Begin To WEEP...*For Your Enemies (Jer. 48:35-36)!* Moab was an enemy to God and His people, but look at how He feels about that nation. It's amazing! God has compassion for EVERYBODY...even those who hate Him! Not so with us. We want God to "Fry" them! *Yet Jesus reminds us to love our enemies and pray for them...just like He does (Matt. 5:43-45)!*

4. You'd Acquire a "Healthy" FEAR of God (Jer. 32:40-41)! I know this isn't popular in some circles, but God isn't just another one of your good-old "Buddies!" Sure Jesus is the Gentle Shepherd...but He's also the Awesome Judge of the World! *Israel learned that God can love and sternly discipline too. That's a lesson all Christians need to learn (Heb. 12:5-17)!*

5. You'd Learn That Anybody Can Return To God...*But You CAN'T Come Back On Your OWN TERMS (Jer. 15:19)!* Israel had two things working in them...Divine Grace and Destructive Sin! *The requirement of restoration is to extract the precious from the vile!* Yes, God will forgive you and receive you back to Himself again. But there is something He requires of you... *Walk Away From a Life of Sin and Trust in His Grace (John 8:11)!*

So there you have it...glimpses of the Heart of God from Jeremiah's pen. Here's the question: *"If God let you step into His heart, what would you do?"* Can He trust you with His heart or will you just shake your head and walk away? *If you open your heart to God's heart, it will become a "Divine Compass" that guides and guards your Destiny in Him!* Sad to say...most people can't handle that kind of trust!

What is God's Spirit Saying to Me...
As I Navigate Life According To Jeremiah

LAMENTATIONS

Postmortem of a Destiny
They Played the Fool!

Have you ever known someone who "Played the Fool" with their life and wasted their future with God? What Happened? Where Did They Go Wrong? ***Don't miss this teaching...it's a matter of Life or Death!***

- What is a "Spiritual Postmortem?"

- Five amazing Discoveries that Jeremiah made about Israel's demise.

- But what if I've already "Played the Fool"...is there any hope for me?

Postmortem of a Destiny
They Played the Fool!

An Autopsy is gruesome. But it's essential if you're going to discover why a person died. A "Spiritual Postmortem" is also a grisly examination...but if you don't do it, you'll never discover why a divine Destiny died! And if you don't know what happened, you could travel down that same road...even to destruction! Jeremiah was a personal witness to the death of his nation's destiny. *As he wrote this Postmortem (called the book of Lamentations) he wept bitterly over WHAT COULD HAVE BEEN!*

Jeremiah's heart was utterly broken and distraught. Through eyes blurred with tears, he saw his beloved city reduced to dust and rubble. The glorious Temple, once the site of sacred worship and joyous celebrations, had been desecrated and stripped of its treasures. Oh the carnage! The young and old alike were slaughtered, maimed or dragged away in chains. Over 800 years earlier, Moses had warned Israel of the fearful consequences of forsaking their covenant (Deut. 28). Now, all those terrible curses were being fulfilled. *Jeremiah mourned over what Judah could have been in God's Kingdom.* But wait! This doesn't have to happen to you! If you learn from Israel's tragedy, you can avoid your own!

> 1st Postmortem Discovery: *It Was a Horrible Death!* No, this was no natural death. It was brutal, vicious and cruel beyond words (Lam. 1:1; 5:10-16)! If you forsake the Lord, your hedge of protection is GONE and you're at the mercy of your enemies...who have NO MERCY! *Learn the lesson well, my friend. Accountability to God is REAL (Rom. 14:10-12)!*

> 2nd Postmortem Discovery: *It Was a Senseless Death!* Israel didn't die nobly or honorably in battle. It was her foolish sins and lack of true leadership that brought this calamity upon her (Lam. 1:5; Jer.

2:8). Amazingly, she never once considered what her actions would do to her Destiny (Lam.1:9)! *Think about it before you depart from God's ways. It will cost you your very soul (Matt. 16:26)!*

3rd Postmortem Discovery: *Insult Was Added To Injury!* The horror of Israel's spiritual death wasn't all that happened. She became the laughing stock of the nations (Lam. 2:15-17)! Israel embarrassed the cause of God and gave His enemies an opportunity to mock the favor and grace He gave her! *Before you do something foolish, remember who you represent and who will be embarrassed by your actions (Philip. 2:15)!*

4th Postmortem Discovery: *But There Was A Glimmer of Hope...Repentance!* As Israel was being carried away, she cried out to the Lord (Lam. 2:19; 3:39-41, 55-58)! Yes, the consequences of sin are indeed severe but they're not forever...if you call upon the Lord! Don't grow angry or bitter when you suffer for your sins. *God is merciful to those who repent with humility (James 4:4-10)!*

5th Postmortem Discovery: *Israel's Tragedy Had a Good Ending...God Gave Her Another Chance To Live!* What an amazingly compassionate God we serve (Lam. 3:21-25, 31-33)! Even as Israel was suffering for her foolishness, God gave her the promise of hope. *Listen carefully to the end of this story. God will restore your Destiny...when you return to Him (Lam. 5:21; Jer. 29:10-14)!*

And that, my friend, is how you Navigate Your Life according to the book of Lamentations. *"But that's the Old Testament,"* you might say, *"I'm a New Testament believer!"* Okay, then read Matt. 7:22-27 and Luke 16:19-31 to discover what Jesus said about accountability. Don't Play the Fool with your Destiny! But in case you have...your only hope is Jesus! *For after you've suffered for your foolishness and if your heart is right, He can restore the Destiny you wasted...just like He did for Peter (Luke 22:31-32)!*

What is God's Spirit Saying to Me...
As I Navigate Life According To Lamentations

EZEKIEL

Feeling Trapped?
Don't Let Frustration Drown Out God!

Ever felt so Frustrated that you didn't even want to hear what God has to say? Israel did. And Ezekiel was the voice of God they didn't want to hear. *If you're feeling trapped, this teaching is for you!*

- Why is it so hard to hear from God when you're Frustrated?
- What was it that Israel didn't want to hear?
- Five things God wants you to know when you feel Trapped and Frustrated.

Feeling Trapped?
Don't Let Frustration Drown Out God!

Circumstances can speak louder than God...*If You Let Them!* This can be especially true when you feel trapped in a situation beyond your control...like Israel was in Babylon. But for you, it might be financial bondage, a dead-end job or a hurtful relationship. The sound of your misery and frustration can be deafening! It can fill your senses to such an extent that you can't think clearly, much less hear from God. The tendency is to either act rashly to remove the pain or to tune out everything...including wise counsel and the voice of the Lord. That's what happened to Israel during their Babylonian captivity. *They couldn't hear God's voice speaking through His prophet because of their misery and distress!*

The prophet Ezekiel was <u>NOT</u> popular with his people. Though he was a fellow prisoner of war with Israel in Babylon, he spoke sobering words they didn't expect or want to hear. He condemned their foolishness and the false leaders who had influenced them. He told them their sufferings in captivity could not be avoided! *He told them that God had a purpose beyond their crisis...but they refused to listen (Ezek. 12:2).* Furthermore, he told them they were stuck in their misery until that season in their history was complete. For this reason they hated the prophet. According to Jewish historians, he was killed by the very people to whom he was sent! *His message was just more than they could handle.*

The reason for Israel's bondage may not be the same as yours, but the principles concerning how to handle distress are the same. *When you feel trapped by life's circumstances, you need to know how to navigate life. Listen to the prophetic words of Ezekiel:*

1. Don't Try to <u>Interpret</u> Your Distress Without Understanding From God. This was Ezekiel's assignment, but they wouldn't

listen (Ezek. 2:4-7). When troubles arise, the tendency is to blame everyone else for your problems...including God! But the Lord knows that stress surfaces hidden character flaws. *When God interprets your crisis, He opens your heart to Him and refines your faith (1 Pet. 1:6-7).*

2. Remember, Your Dark Experience Is <u>Seasonal</u>. Some circumstances have to run their course...you can't hurry them up or make them go away! Begin to view your "Dark" experience as God's "Light" shining into your life. Light exposes and purges. *Once the season of purging is complete, God has a glorious future just waiting for you to step into (Luke 22:31-32).*

3. Listen to the <u>Watchmen</u> God Assigns to You. Ezekiel was a divine trumpet sounding an alarm from God (Ezek. 3:17-21). When God sees trouble coming in your life, He assigns godly men and women to speak warnings to you. *Don't ignore or kill the prophet who brings God's words of caution to you. If you do, it's like jumping over a guardrail at the Grand Canyon!*

4. God Never Forgets His <u>Covenant</u> With You...And Neither Should You! God reminded His people of the Covenant He made with them during their youth (Ezek. 16:60-63). When trouble distracts you, it's easy to forget the original relationship you had with the Lord. *Remember and return to that sweet moment when God first met with you and touched your heart with His love.*

5. Your Valley of "Dry Bones" Will Live...When <u>God's Spirit</u> Breathes On You! Israel's dilemma was described in Ezekiel's vision: a slain army with dead men's bones scattered and dry-rotted (Ezek. 37:1-14). All hope was gone...until God showed up! *All it takes is one breath of God's Spirit into your spiritual lungs and His life returns to you again.* <u>*You can't live without God...and Neither Can Your Destiny!*</u>

Always keep the "Map" of Ezekiel <u>**CLOSE**</u> to your heart. It reminds you that there really is a road out of your troubles. Always keep the "Compass" of God's Spirit <u>**IN**</u> your heart. *He points the way out of your troubles and into your Restored Destiny in Him.*

What is God's Spirit Saying to Me...
As I Navigate Life According To Ezekiel

DANIEL

Faith Crisis: Lord, if You Don't Show Up... I'm Toast!

Remember Daniel in the Lion's Den? Remember his three friends in the Fiery Furnace? These are great men who stayed true to God when their Faith was challenged. But what about you? *Could YOU handle a Crisis in Your Faith...at work or even in the church?*

- What is a "Faith Crisis?"
- How does Mature Faith deal with challenges to your beliefs and your life?
- How can you grow into Mature Faith and be able to stand up to this kind of crisis?

Faith Crisis: Lord, if You Don't Show Up... I'm Toast!

"Toast" was <u>literally</u> what Shadrach, Meshach and Abed-nego were about to become. *If God didn't show up in a hurry, they would be thrown into a burning fiery furnace!* Their ego-crazed "boss" (King Nebuchadnezzar) had demanded that his "employees" (his subjects) treat him as if he were God! Brashly he screamed out, *"Who is the god who will deliver you from my hands?"* Listen to the response of their faith: *"Our God whom we serve* <u>IS ABLE</u> *to deliver us from the burning fiery furnace, and* <u>HE WILL</u> *deliver us from your hand, O king.* <u>BUT IF NOT</u>, *let it be known to you, O king, that we do not serve your gods, nor will we worship the gold image which you have set up" (Dan. 3:17-18).* These three, along with Daniel, were prisoners of war with Israel in Babylon. Daniel, the main character in this prophetic book of the Bible, had a similar experience. *Had God not shown up...he would have been Lion Food!*

A crisis is a turning point in a person's life. In medicine, it's a turning point for better or worse when a person is suffering from a life-threatening disease or fever. In American History, the Revolutionary War erupted when colonists reached a crisis point...liberty from England or death! *In your spiritual life, Faith is* <u>belief in God, who He is</u> *and* <u>what He does</u>. *A "Faith Crisis" is a decisive event (a turning point) in your walk with God that determines whether you live or die spiritually.* Like Daniel and his three friends, unless you have sufficient faith (Mature Faith) to deal with this kind of crisis, you will certainly die! Here's how Mature Faith helps you navigate your life and Destiny in God:

1. When Your Core Beliefs and Relationship With God Are Threatened...*You Need <u>MATURE</u> Faith!* Like Daniel and his friends, your faith in God and His word are non-negotiable. When life comes to an end, you'll stand before the <u>Lord</u> to

give an account for how you've lived...not your boss or your preacher. *Regardless who tries to make you believe or do something contrary to what you know is Biblical Truth...Don't believe it and don't do it!*

2. When Faced With Life or Death Issues Beyond Your Control...*You Need* **MATURE** *Faith.* Listen again to what Shadrach, Meshach and Abed-nego said, *"Our God whom we serve **IS ABLE** to deliver us!"* Never question God's ability. He spoke the universe into existence and His infinite power can do anything! *Sure, God may choose to use skilled professionals or doctors to work through, but in the end, it's His sovereign power that makes it happen.*

3. When You Lack Confidence in God's Willingness to Help You...*You Need* **MATURE** *Faith.* Daniel's friends were fully convinced that God's ultimate intention was to rescue them. *"And **HE WILL** deliver us from your hand!"* was their bold retort to Nebuchadnezzar. It's one thing to know that God can, but it makes all the difference in the world to believe that He will. *You serve an infinitely powerful God...and He is infinitely compassionate toward you (Mark 1:40-42)!*

4. But **MATURE** Faith Is Never Presumptuous. There's a delicate balance between **Believing** in God's deliverance and **Demanding** that He do it! Don't forget these men also said, *"BUT IF NOT!"* What'cha gonna do if God doesn't show up the way you expect? Some people get angry with God and others totally throw away their faith. God didn't answer Paul's prayers the way he wanted (2 Cor. 12:7-10). Even Jesus had to relinquish His will to God (Matt. 26:39). *I'd rather be "Toast" than lose out with God! But when you hold on to Him...He'll never let go of you!*

I'm emphasizing **"MATURE"** Faith because not all faith is the same. Jesus chided His disciples for having "Little" Faith...faith that didn't meet the magnitude of their crisis (Matt. 6:30; 8:26; 14:30-31; 16:8). *So, how do you get Mature Faith? It grows into maturity through the knowledge of God's word (Rom. 10:17), the testing of your faith (James. 1:2-5) and the power of His grace (1 Pet. 5:10).*

What is God's Spirit Saying to Me...
As I Navigate Life According To Daniel

HOSEA

Does God Still Love Me...
After What I Did?

Two things constantly amaze me: *1) The fallen natures in people that run from the God who created and loves them; 2) The intense love that God has for people who run away from His love!*

- What's the story of Hosea and how does it relate to my life?
- A real-life answer to the question, "Does God Still Love Me?"
- Seven amazing offers from God...Don't take these lightly!

Does God Still Love Me... After What I Did?

There she was...the wayward wife of the great prophet Hosea, shamed, disgraced and standing on an auction block being sold as a common slave. Beyond belief, she had left the arms of her husband and went to the streets. We don't know the gory details, but she may have become a temple prostitute, another man's concubine, or a street harlot. The pain in Hosea's heart must have been unbearable as he looked upon the woman he once loved...years had passed, beauty now gone, totally undesirable. You won't believe what Hosea did next. **He bought her and restored her as his wife again (Hosea 1-3)!** *"What a heart-warming story,"* some may say after reading this amazing account. This, my friend, is no Hollywood script...it's a real story. *It's **God's** story! It's **YOUR** story! It's the tragedy of how we exchange God's love for the emptiness of sin. But more importantly, it's the glorious story of Redemption...how God, in His everlasting love, paid the ultimate price to redeem you and me from sin and draw us back to Himself!*

Someone, right now, is reading this teaching and saying, *"But pastor, you don't know the terrible things I've done. I've wasted my life and there's nothing about me that God or anyone else could love."* You're right...I don't know who you are or what you've done with your life. But this I do know...***God loves you more than you can possibly imagine. In fact, He loves you more than you love yourself!*** Even as God loved Israel, who went after false gods and prostituted herself with foolish living, God loves you and reaches out to you...***time after time! Listen to His amazing offer in Hosea 2:19-20:***

1. I Will Betroth You <u>FOREVER</u>. Forever means now, in the future and after you die! Forever is a covenant so intense that God never breaks it. *Compare this with all your other "lovers" who draw your attention away from God!*

2. I Will Betroth You To Me In <u>RIGHTEOUSNESS</u>. This means that the covenant God offers to you will make you righteous, holy and pure in Him. *Compare this with the shame that others bring upon you!*

3. I Will Betroth You To Me In <u>JUSTICE</u>. Justice means that God governs your life in fairness, integrity and without partiality. *Compare this to the way cheap relationships treat you!*

4. I Will Betroth You To Me In <u>LOVINGKINDNESS</u>. God is kind and shows goodness to you...regardless of how you've ignored His love. *Compare this to others who say, "I love you" but don't really mean it!*

5. I Will Betroth You To Me In <u>MERCY</u>. God has compassion for you when you fail. With tender love He reaches out to restore you. *Compare this to your "lovers" who belittle and hurt you!*

6. I Will Betroth You To Me In <u>FAITHFULNESS</u>. Faithfulness means God is steadfast in His love and commitment to you. *Compare this to those who are here today and gone tomorrow!*

7. And You Shall <u>KNOW</u> The Lord. This is the intimate sharing of lives. God opens His heart to you and you open your soul to Him...forever joined. *Compare this to being used and discarded!*

Now it's time for you to choose. Will you settle for the temporary or the eternal? However, there's one "little" catch to this story if you want a happy ending. **God expects you to RESPOND to His Offer.** Unfortunately, Israel didn't! She refused to listen to God's voice through the prophet and she was taken away into Assyrian captivity...forever! Listen to God's voice speaking to you through this teaching, my friend. *Does God Still Love You? You Can't Imagine How Much! Navigate your life by responding to His infinite love and incredibly gracious offer. And when you do, He'll buy you back and make you His wife...forever!*

What is God's Spirit Saying to Me...
As I Navigate Life According To Hosea

JOEL

In the Midst of Your Biggest Mess... God Gives Hope!

Life is precarious. All it takes is one Big Mistake...and your career, family, future and ministry is ruined forever! Do you know anybody like this? *If so, this teaching is a Must Read!*

- I've heard that all Old Testament Prophets declare Doom and Judgment. Is that true?
- Why would God promise good things to people who belligerently rebel against Him?
- Four Promises from God that help navigate your life toward your Divine Destiny.

In the Midst of Your Biggest Mess... God Gives Hope!

Ever "mess up" big time...I mean REALLY BIG? I'm talking about a life-changing, career-busting, family-destroying, ministry-gutting, ship-sinking personal mess up that forever shatters your future beyond repair. Sure, it happens every day...to <u>other</u> people. You read about them in the newspaper, hear about them on the radio and see them on television. **But if it happens to <u>YOU</u>...it seems like the end of the world!** As you look back across the wreckage caused by foolishness, you can't imagine any good that lies ahead of you. *But GOD DOES!* Listen to the incredible story of what happened in the book of Joel.

Israel had been ripped in two...the northern kingdom of Israel and the southern kingdom of Judah (1 Kings 11:11; 12:16-17). The northern kingdom had been swept away for their apostasy, belligerent rebellion against God and refusal to repent. Tragically, Judah was headed in the same direction of corruption; except for one thing...they held to the hope that God gave through the prophet Joel. *Incredibly, in the midst of their mess, God gave them a promise of a glorious future...<u>IF</u> they would just return to Him with a repentant heart.* Now here's the point of this teaching...that promise includes you and me as well! Listen to these amazing **"Navigational Promises"** found in the book of Joel:

1. God Does <u>NOT</u> Want To Punish You. Listen to His heart as He entreated Judah to repent, *"Return to the Lord your God, For He is gracious and merciful, slow to anger, and of great kindness; and He relents from doing harm" (Joel 2:13).* Like a loving parent, God embraces the child He disciplines. *What does God really want? His ultimate desire is for you to share in His holiness (Heb. 12:10-11).*

2. Repentance Starts in Your <u>HEART</u>! Repentance is more than just "saying" I'm sorry or feeling that God has "forced" you to

change. It's a deep heart-experience (Ps. 51:17) in which your actions bring you to such godly sorrow that you'll do whatever is necessary to change (Joel 2:13; 2 Cor. 7:10). *If your heart isn't broken when you sin, you're experiencing Spiritual Heart-Failure!*

3. God Promises to <u>RESTORE</u> All That You've Lost...After Your Heart Truly Repents. Though Judah belligerently turned away from the Lord, read His gracious promise of restoration in Joel 2:21-27. Does that mean if I repent, God is "indebted" to restore what I've lost? Absolutely NOT! *What an amazing God! He gives the repentant sinner what he does <u>NOT</u> deserve...Mercy and Restoration!*

4. Now Here's God's Greatest Promise of All...<u>HIS SPIRIT</u> (Joel 2:28-29)! Why would God give His precious Spirit to a people who rebel against Him? Because He has compassion on our pitiful plight in life (Ps. 103:8-14). The Holy Spirit is God's Agent of Restoration (Ps. 51:11-13). *God knows that without the power of His Spirit, you can't return to Him at all. It's His Spirit who draws you to Jesus and shows you His salvation (John 16:13-14).*

So, how can you navigate your Destiny according to these promises? Listen to the definition of "Promise" from the New Bible Dictionary:

"God's Promise is a word that goes forth into unfilled time. It reaches ahead of its speaker and its recipient, to mark an appointment between them in the future. Unlike men, God knows and commands the future!"

This means the Lord will not forsake you. He'll walk with you <u>through</u> the consequences of your failure and will preserve your original Destiny in Him. This means you have HOPE...even in the midst of your biggest mess! *Navigate your life back to God, my friend, by using the "Map" of His Word and by following the "Compass" of His Spirit.*

Then the end of your life will be better than the beginning (Eccles. 7:8; Rom. 8:28).

What is God's Spirit Saying to Me...
As I Navigate Life According To Joel

AMOS

Amos WHO?
Why God Likes to Use Ordinary People

In all nations and cultures of the earth there's a dichotomy of two opposing groups of people...the **"Ordinary"** class and the **"Ruling"** class. ***But guess who God uses to correct who?***

- Who was the prophet Amos? An <u>Ordinary</u> person with an <u>Extraordinary</u> ministry.

- Why does God like to use <u>Ordinary</u> people to do His work in the earth?

- Three ways to navigate your life as an <u>Ordinary</u> person.

Amos WHO?
Why God Likes to Use Ordinary People

I can just imagine what people might have said when Amos, an "ordinary" sheepherder and farmer, stepped up and began to prophesy. It might have sounded something like this, *"Sure, you're a respected business person in your community, but a "prophet"... I DON'T THINK SO! Who are YOU to speak for God and tell US what to do? We're the ones who are in charge...NOT you! Now just go on about your business and leave us alone!"*

And they were right! Amos was not a famous spiritual leader before he began to prophesy. **But when the Lord spoke to his heart, he roared like a lion (Amos 3:8)!** He threw off the covers and exposed the hypocritical lives of the rich and famous and their atrocities against the poor. Nobody who disregarded God's Laws was safe from his prophetic "scalpel." It sliced open the rottenness of a society that oppressed and defrauded the helpless, causing them to sell themselves and their children into slavery. Even religious leaders who aligned themselves with the corrupt ruling class were severely judged by God (Amos 7:10-17). **Yes, Amos was like a lion...God's voice roaring against a world of pain and injustice.**

So why does the Lord like to use ORDINARY people to do His work? Consider this:

1. **God Puts to Shame Those Who Are "Strong."** If a mighty man changes society, his fame and pride will increase. But if God uses the weak and insignificant to proclaim His "plumb line," all will know it's the Lord, not a man, who brings God's righteous standard (Amos 7:8; 1 Cor. 1:27-29).

2. **God Exalts Those Who Are "Little" in Their Own Eyes.** If you want God to fight against you, let your heart become lifted

up (James 4:6). If you want God to lift you up, humble yourself before Him (1 Peter 5:6). Humble people know who they ARE and who they are NOT (Amos 7:14-15).

3. **God Shifts the Emphasis from the "Leadership" to His People.** Eph. 4:11-16 sets the record straight. Spiritual leaders are NOT to be center stage in ministry...YOU are! Their assignment is to equip, train and release God's people to represent Christ to a lost and suffering world.

4. **Ordinary People Are "Touched" by the Struggles of Suffering Humanity.** Even religious leaders in Amos' day had joined themselves to the insulated world of affluent rulers. Not so with ordinary people like you, me and Amos. God uses us because we experience the pain of the world and know what it takes to heal the wounds. *Read James 2:1-17 to see how God wants you to "Keep it Real" in your faith.*

"Okay," you might say, *"This is all well and good, but how does this help me navigate my life toward my Destiny?"*

1. **Just Be You!** Don't try to pattern your life after some "famous" person. You're already famous...in God's eyes! *He's gifted and destined you to do good things for Him (Eph. 2:10).*

2. **Guard Yourself Against Pride.** Resist the temptation to tell everybody, *"Look what God did through ME!"* That's pride, my friend. *The end of that road is destruction (Prov. 16:18)!*

3. **Expect an Extraordinary God to Work Through You.** "Ordinary" doesn't mean God won't do amazing things through you. Listen to God's voice and "roar" against injustice in the world where you live. *But remember, God's strong words always end with HOPE (Amos 9:13-15)!*

What is God's Spirit Saying to Me...
As I Navigate Life According To Amos

OBADIAH

I Don't Like This Book!
It Doesn't Make Me Happy!

It's amazing that some Christians ignore many Old Testament books...especially the prophets. I guess they don't want to hear about God's "Other Side." *But wait till you hear the "Good News" in Obadiah!*

- What do you mean: God's "Other Side?"
- Why did God speak so harshly against a country called Edom?
- Four essential ways to navigate your life from Obadiah...the shortest book in the Old Testament.

I Don't Like This Book!
It Doesn't Make Me Happy!

News Flash! God doesn't exist to make you happy! Sure, He's merciful, patient and kind...but He's also infinitely righteous and just. When God sees persistent evil working in unrepentant people, He warns them over and over. But if they refuse His warnings, He'll eventually execute judgment, destroy wickedness and replace it with His righteousness. *This is what some call God's "Other Side."* People don't like it. They would much rather enjoy His mercy and kindness. That's why they don't want to read Obadiah. But it's true nevertheless. *So why did Obadiah condemn Edom and declare its destruction?*

Remember Esau? You know...Jacob's brother, the guy that traded his inheritance for a bowl of stew? If you read the story again in Gen. 25:29-34, you'll discover that Esau had absolutely no respect for his birthright. That birthright was more than the earthly possessions of his father Isaac. It was his dad's spiritual inheritance...even his faith and relationship with the Living God! Thus Esau warred against Jacob (who became Israel) and the God that Israel served. *Nine hundred years later, Esau's descendants occupied the land called Edom. Tragically they remained just like their forefather...godless and immoral (Heb. 12:16-17)!* Throughout history they purposely did everything in their power to bring harm to God's people and ignore them when they were in trouble (Obad. 10-14). *God does not delight in the death of the wicked (Ezek. 18:23), but when the wicked refuse to repent..judgment is certain!*

Therefore, the "Other Side" of God is just as real as His mercy, patience and kindness. How then shall you navigate your life to fulfill your destiny in Him? Consider this:

1. **Don't Think That God's Judgment Is Just an Old Testament Concept.** There's a tendency, even among Christians, to

disregard that part of God's character they don't like. They forget the strong words Jesus spoke about those who practice lawlessness and show no mercy (Matt. 7:21-23; 25:32-46). Or maybe they didn't read that God really does judge unbelief (Rom. 11:22-23)?

2. **Use the Law of Sowing and Reaping for Your Good!** Obadiah declared that Edom would reap the same violence and cruelty they dished out to Israel (Obad. 15). God is not partial concerning this truth; it works regardless of who you are. *But here's the "Flip Side:" If you sow to the Spirit, you'll reap eternal life...as long as you don't grow weary in doing good (Gal. 6:7-9)!*

3. **Caution! An Evil Spirit Lies Behind Generational Pride and Arrogance.** Sure, Esau was an evil person...but his ancestors didn't have to follow his wicked pattern (Obad. 3)! *If you find yourself arrogantly angry and wanting to get even with people your fore parents hated, you're following Satan's pattern of pride (1 Tim. 3:6)!* Leave vengeance to God, my friend (Heb. 10:30-31).

4. **But Here's the Good News...You're Not Edom!** The Old Testament story is about how God rescues those who humble themselves, call upon His name and trust in His salvation. The Old is a foreshadowing of the New as it anticipates the coming Messiah who will save His people from their sins. *Jesus is that Messiah and you are His people (1 Pet. 2:9-10)! That means when you belong to Jesus, you have passed out of judgment into eternal life (John 5:24).* Sure, you have to renounce sin and walk in God's light...but your salvation is based on what Jesus did for you, not on your own personal righteousness!

So, my friend, what do you think of the book of Obadiah now? Is it about gloom, doom and judgment? Not for you it isn't...if you belong to Jesus. And that's why the Gospel is called "Good News!" *Use*

Obadiah as a divine "Map" that shows you how to avoid the error of Edom. And follow the "Compass" of the Holy Spirit as He points you to Jesus...the One who qualifies you for your Destiny in God.

What is God's Spirit Saying to Me...
As I Navigate Life According To Obadiah

JONAH

What if God Showed Mercy... To the Person You Hate Most?

Ever been hurt by someone who tried to destroy you? *Want them to suffer for what they did? Hey, you're in good company...so did Jonah!*

- Everybody's heard about Jonah and the Big Fish. But you may not know the Rest of the Story!
- How God turned the tables on Israel and Jonah...and us too!
- How can Jonah's dramatic story help you to navigate your life?

What if God Showed Mercy...
To the Person You Hate Most?

"That no-good, sorry, blankety-blank, two-timing, deceiving jerk! I hope God really teaches him a lesson or two!" Do you know anyone who fits that description? Maybe it's your "ex" that ran off with your best friend, skipped the country and child-support too? Or could it be that dictatorial boss that makes you work overtime while he takes his girlfriend on a two-week Mediterranean Cruise and pays you peanuts! Perhaps it's your so-called "friend" and co-worker who undermined your confidence, squealed to the boss and got that big promotion you really wanted? **Would it surprise you to learn that the prophet Jonah felt the same way you do about people he didn't like?** It was the Assyrians living in the capital city of Nineveh that he hoped God would punish. *The LAST thing Jonah wanted was for the Lord to show mercy to the brutal enemies of Israel!* Here's what happened:

Israel's northern kingdom was in deep trouble with God. Their belligerent rebellion had reached heaven and the Lord sent warning after warning through His prophets. If they would not repent, they would be swept away by the cruelest and most dreaded nation in the Middle East...Assyria (Hosea 11:5-7). **Can you imagine how Jonah felt when God told him to bring a message of God's mercy to Nineveh, the most important city in Assyria?** Jonah ran the other way as fast as he could (Jonah 1:1-3)! He hated Assyria and wanted them to suffer for what they were about to do to Israel! So what did God do? He chastened Jonah in a way that he would never forget. God caused a great fish to swallow him alive! When the prophet finally obeyed and went to Nineveh, guess what happened? **Sure enough, they repented. With great compassion, the Lord spared them from destruction. So what did Jonah do next?** *He got offended at what God did!*

"Great Story!" you might say, *"But how does this help me navigate my life toward my Destiny?"* Consider this:

1. We Don't Have a Clue...*As to How God Thinks.* The book of Jonah is an amazing message of God's love that gives people opportunities to repent and return to Him. He loves the entire human race and doesn't want any to perish...including the person who hurt you the most! Remember who you are, my friend. God calls you to represent Jesus to a lost world. *If you really want to think like God, pray for your enemies. Ask Him to forgive the person who is destroying you, just like Jesus did in Luke 23:34!*

2. Even "Great" Men and Women of God...*Can Be Wrong!* Of all the people who I thought would understand God's work in the world, it would be His prophets. But not so with Jonah. Remember, "Greatness" is not the person himself; it's GOD in the person! Regardless of the Lord's call on your life, if you don't THINK like God, you can't represent Him properly. *Don't allow anger and prejudice to hinder you from fulfilling the Lord's destiny for your life (Rom. 12:17-21).*

3. God Honors True Repentance...*Even If It's From Your Enemies!* Perhaps you've forgotten..."ALL have sinned and fall short of the glory of God" (Rom. 3:23). YOU were once an enemy of God, but He gave you an amazing opportunity to repent...while you were still in sin (Rom. 5:6-10)! *And so, dear heart, why wouldn't you want your enemies to repent as well? Hmm...Good Question!*

4. If Our Enemies Can Repent...*So Should We!* Jonah is a story of Repentance. Israel was about to be swept away by Assyria for their Lack of Repentance. To drive the point home, God showed them how their enemies repented when they heard Jonah's preaching. This point was so powerful that Jesus used it to condemn the Unrepentant Religious Leaders of His day (Matt. 12:41).

What then does Jonah's "Map" show you? *It's a clear message that your Destiny in God depends on changing (repenting from) merciless attitudes concerning others...even those who hurt you (Matt. 5:43-45).* Now all you have to do is to allow the "Compass" of God's Spirit to lead you into that repentance.

What is God's Spirit Saying to Me...
As I Navigate Life According To Jonah

MICAH

The Remnant
God's "Redemption Island" Survivors

Ever wonder why you survived a horrible past and others didn't? Do you think that maybe, just maybe, God has a purpose in mind? ***Well, You're Right...He Does!***

- Who are God's Remnant People?
- Why did YOU survive your experiences?
- Five questions that will determine if you are part of God's Remnant or not.

The Remnant
God's "Redemption Island" Survivors

Redemption Island was a new twist producers came up with for the Survivor reality TV show. People who were eliminated had one more chance to get back in the game. Well, God had a "Redemption Island" program 3,000 years ago! It's called "The Remnant." And it's not a game show...it's Reality!

Israel was rushing headlong into apostasy and corruption. *They had mixed world religions into their faith and their leaders refused to heed God's warnings.* Thus God had no other alternative but to back away and allow them to be swept away by their brutal enemies. This was the message of the prophet Micah. But, like all true prophets of God, Micah's message also included a merciful glimmer of hope...A FEW WOULD BE SAVED! God called them His Remnant...a redeemed few whom He rescued from the fallen masses and restored to their divine Destinies in Him.

This was true for Israel and it's true for families and churches as well. You may have grown up in a dysfunctional family intent on self-destruction. **Yet somehow you survived it!** Or you could have been part of a once great ministry that imploded with internal failures. **But somehow you were rescued from it!** Why? Because God purposes to have a people whose hearts belong to Him (2 Chron. 16:9). Maybe He saw something in you that He could rescue. Perhaps it was just His sovereign choice. But whatever the reason, you were shown unbelievable mercy as He rescued you, brought you to Himself and claimed you as His own (1 Pet. 2:9-10).

God's Remnant people are those whom He rescues out of the midst of sin, corruption and apostasy by the saving grace of His Son, Jesus. They are the ones who respond to His mercy with hearts of gratitude.

So, are you part of God's Remnant? Here's a **Spiritual Questionnaire** for you to consider:

1. Have You <u>SURVIVED</u> the Total Collapse of Your Family or Church? I'm talking about a miraculous rescue that wasn't your ability to "outwit, outplay or outlast." You knew it was the work of God (Micah 4:5-7)! *Amazingly, He kept you from throwing away your faith in God's true family or His true Church during that collapse.* If this is you, then you're part of God's Remnant People.

2. Has God Given You <u>WISDOM</u> From Your Experience? God's discipline always results in wisdom...if your heart is open (Ps. 119:67, 71). *The Lord uses your difficult experiences to teach you valuable lessons in life.* If this is you, then you're part of God's Remnant People.

3. Are You a Recipient of God's Great <u>COMPASSION</u> and <u>FORGIVENESS</u>? None of us are guiltless. None deserve His mercy or restoring love. *When He passes over our rebellion and pardons our iniquities, we are forever grateful and choose to serve Him all the days of our lives.* If this is you, then you're part of God's Remnant People (Micah 7:18-19).

4. Can You Turn Your Experiences Into <u>ENCOURAGEMENT</u> For Others? Why does God extend His hand of unmerited favor to us? Because of who He is and because of what He desires us to do for others. *If you can encourage others who are going through the same difficulties as you experienced, then you're part of God's Remnant People (Micah 5:7).*

5. Has This Experience Caused You to be a <u>WARRIOR</u> for Righteousness? If there's any positive result that can come from sin, it's that once you've been delivered from its grip, you can war against it with a righteous fervor. No, you don't war

against people, but you help them to escape as you did. *If this is you, then you're part of God's Remnant People (Micah 5:8).*

And that's how you Navigate Your Life according to Micah. Recognize that God has rescued you for a higher purpose than you realize. Then begin to act like His Remnant people...a witness of God's Greatness and an influence for others to achieve their Destiny in Him.

What is God's Spirit Saying to Me...
As I Navigate Life According To Micah

NAHUM

Divine Justice
When Bad Guys Get What's Coming to Them!

It's called Divine Justice...God's law of sowing and reaping that stops evil people in their tracks. But what happens in your heart when Bad Guys get what's coming to them? ***Better read this!***

- How does God decide who's a Good Guy and who's a Bad Guy? What happens to them?
- Can a Bad Guy become a Good Guy?
- Three ways the book of Nahum helps you to navigate your Destiny in God.

Divine Justice
When Bad Guys Get What's Coming to Them!

Do you like movies where Good Guys win and Bad Guys lose? I do! Sure, there's way too much violence, but we live in a world of extreme brutality and cruelty. Evil people intent on hurting the weak, taking from the defenseless and killing the innocent don't hesitate to randomly inflict pain on others. It's interesting that all successful movies and novels have a hated villain that needs to be stopped. **Now where do you think Hollywood gets the idea that good should triumph over evil?** *It's written in the heart of God!* Though these producers and directors may not know the Lord, they know what draws viewers and makes money. It's when justice prevails and the bad guys get what's coming to them! That's exactly what the book of Nahum is all about. Let's take a look at this book of **Divine Justice**.

Remember the story of Jonah and where God sent him to preach? That's right...it was to the violent and cruel people of Nineveh, the capital of Assyria. Remember what happened? They repented and the Lord spared them from destruction. But guess what happened a few generations later? *They forgot God's mercy and grace toward their nation.* Driven by pride, power and self-indulgence, they brutally attacked Israel, pillaged their cities and shed blood indiscriminately (Nahum 3:1-3). Their atrocities reached heaven and crossed an unalterable line with God. In three short chapters, the prophet Nahum leveled God's holy judgment upon these ruthless people (Nahum 3:4-7). *Nahum's message was short and simple...the "Bad Guys" of Assyria would experience the full weight of God's Divine Justice!*

So, who are the "Good Guys" and "Bad Guys" and what happens to them?

1. Good Guys Aren't Sinless...*But They Trust a Merciful God and Seek His Forgiveness!* After David's adulterous affair with

Bathsheba and his senseless murder of her husband, he wrote Psalm 32 and 51. *Read what David wrote and you'll see how "Good Guys" handle personal sin!*

2. Bad Guys Trust Only In Themselves...*Their Only God Is Their Own Appetites (Rom. 16:18; Philip. 3:19).* They bow to no one and reject the idea of humility and repentance before the Lord.

3. Good Guys May Not Have an Abundance Now...*But They Will Inherit God's Kingdom in the End (Matt. 5:3; James 2:5)!* Those who give their lives and trust their souls to the Lord will enjoy His unimaginable riches...FOREVER! (Luke 16:19-25).

4. Bad Guys Accumulate Riches and Lands by Treachery...*But They Will Lose it All in the End (Luke 12:16-21)!* How futile it is to amass fortunes through deception and spend eternity in Hell (Matt. 16:26)!

5. <u>BUT</u>, Bad Guys Can Become Good Guys...*If They Truly Humble Their Hearts Before God and Repent!* Our God is amazing! Even the vilest sinner can find mercy with Him (1 Tim. 1:15-16)!

What have you learned from the "Map" of Nahum and how does this help you Navigate your Life with God's Spirit "Compass"?

1. Apostasy Begins by Forgetting God's Past Acts of Grace Toward You! Don't be like Nineveh who forgot the mercies of God. God is patient...but not forever (2 Pet. 3:9-18)!

2. Never Take Your Own Vengeance...Leave That to God (Rom. 12:18-21)! Why? Because when God disciplines people, they can repent. But if you try to get even, the end is always evil!

3. **When Bad Guys Get What's Coming To Them...Weep Over Their Lost Souls (Prov. 24:17)!** Yes, I know...it's hard for me to do that too. But if God lives in us, we have no choice (Ezek. 18:23)!

What is God's Spirit Saying to Me...
As I Navigate Life According To Nahum

HABAKKUK

How to Survive Life...
When Everything Is Falling Apart!

Do you know people whose world is tearing apart at the seams? Some like to blame God and everybody else around them. A few might even dare to blame themselves. ***But what would YOU do?***

- Why do bad things happen to people?
- When the worst happens, is it okay to question God?
- How can people survive the disasters they're in?

How to Survive Life...
When Everything Is Falling Apart!

Have you ever looked into the darkest of nights, shook your head in dismay and asked, *"WHY, Lord?!" "Why are these things happening to me? What am I going to do now? Are You even listening to me?"* For you, it might be a tragic loss, a crumbling marriage, or a threatening illness. For Habakkuk, it was his beloved people who were self-destructing from internal corruption and were about to be swept away by a pagan nation (Hab. 1:1-4). Regardless of the situation, the questions are the same..."WHY?" and "HOW DO I SURVIVE IT?"

Prophets are like you and me...they ask God questions. The difference is that God answers them in very, VERY strange ways! He gives them dreams and visions and tells them to do odd and unusual things to illustrate what He is about to do (Dan. 7:1; Ezek. 4:4; Acts 21:10-11). And so it was with the prophet Habakkuk. His whole world was falling apart and he couldn't do anything about it. All he could do was ask God, *"What's Going On, Here?!"* God's answer: *"I'm about to do something you wouldn't believe!" (Hab. 1:5).* Habakkuk staggered at God's answer to his "WHY" question. Sin, even among God's people, must be confronted (Hab. 1:6). Then in the midst of Habakkuk's dismay, the Lord told him how to survive the horror that was coming, *"The righteous will live by his faith" (Hab. 2:4).* Faith toward God in the midst of tragedy is <u>THE</u> ANSWER! Why? Because it draws God's heart close to you! Here's what FAITH does for you:

1. **FAITH in God Humbles Proud Hearts and Eliminates Blame Shifting.** It's okay for believers to ask God questions, but they must never blame Him or others for their problems. Our sin-riddled world isn't God's fault. It's ours! Corruption in people and even the forces of nature resulted from Adam's failure (Gen. 3). Faith is an act of humility...it confesses that we are

helpless without God! *Faith with a humble heart is a "magnet" for God's grace (James 4:6)!*

2. FAITH Calls Upon God for a Righteous Solution...Regardless of the Consequences. Did Habakkuk want his people to suffer the consequences of sin? Of course not! But he was mature enough to realize there is a place beyond which God's patience will not go. The consequences of sin are painful. But when God gets involved, the end result is righteousness (Heb. 12:6-11; Ps. 119:67, 71). *Faith doesn't run from God's correction; it welcomes it and runs to it!*

3. FAITH is Confident That God Will Judge Evil and Restore You When the Dust Settles! Though God used the Chaldeans to discipline Israel, He would severely judge them for their pride, wickedness and ruthlessness (Hab. 1:7-11). If you're suffering because of evil people, be assured that God will deal with them...without your help! But what will happen to you? *Your faith ensures the Lord will restore you...as long as your heart remains humble (Hab. 3:2, 18).*

4. FAITH in God Sets You on High and Makes You Walk Securely, Even in Dangerous Places. Because of Habakkuk's covenant with God, he knew the Lord was with him, regardless of the horrors that lay before him and his people. Like a deer walking with agility and confidence over treacherous mountain pathways, so will you be in the midst of your darkest hour (Hab. 3:19). *Faith in God gives you unbelievable peace and joy! God is in charge and everything is right!*

How do you survive life when everything is falling apart? The answer is FAITH! *Faith in God through His Son, Jesus, will make you more than a survivor...even more than a conqueror in Him (Rom. 8:37-39)!* Remember, Faith is NOT passive...it's actively believing, hoping and confidently walking with God even in your darkest hour.

What is God's Spirit Saying to Me...
As I Navigate Life According To Habakkuk

ZEPHANIAH

Do "Over-The-Top" Christians Annoy You? Guess What Annoys God?

There are no "new traps"...just old ones that new people keep falling into. Even the early church fell into the same trap that caught Judah. **Want to find out what it was?**

- What are "over-the-top" believers and what do they have to do with this teaching?
- What did the early church have in common with Judah?
- How can you use the truth discovered in Zephaniah to redirect your life?

Do "Over-The-Top" Christians Annoy You? Guess What Annoys God?

Some call them "Charismaniacs." Others refer to them as Fanatics. But God calls them His People! We're talking about flamboyant Christians who love to jump up and down at just the mention of the name of Jesus. They're the ones who stand in line for the church doors to open. They carry their bibles to church, work and even to the Bowling Alley! They feverishly take notes during sermons and love to shout, *"Amen! Preach it, Brother!"* They volunteer for every church project and are the first to come forward when there's an altar call.

What did Judah have in common with "over-the-top" believers? ABSOLUTELY NOTHING! That's why God was so angry with them...they had become complacent and were "stagnant in spirit" (Zeph. 1:12 NASB). And for that reason, they would be utterly destroyed! Judah, the southern kingdom of Israel, had become so apathetic in their faith that they lost all fear of God. *"The Lord neither rewards nor punishes"* was their foolish assumption (Zeph. 1:12 NET). When they needed help, instead of looking to the Lord with humility, they sought false gods and the influence of pagan nations (Zeph. 1:5-8). They were uncorrectable and too prideful to repent (Zeph. 3:2). Therefore, the Lord sent a devastating message through Zephaniah...destruction and judgment would befall the entire nation (Zeph. 1:1-4). But Israel wasn't always like this. At one time they honored God and rejected false religions of the world. What Happened to them? *What happens today that causes Christians to become complacent and non-caring? It's the reoccurring pattern of Judah's slow demise.*

- Their Priests and Prophets Were Reckless and Unholy (Zeph. 3:4 NASB). If leaders mishandle God's word, their foolishness will lead their people into Apostasy...a turning away from the

One True God. *If you're following a leader who leads you away from Biblical Truth...your fate will be like Judah's.*

- **They Became Cynical.** *"Been There; Done That; Got The T-Shirt"* is the slogan of apathy. They figure they've seen all that the church has to offer and are looking for something new and more exciting. *Like some people in the early church, they turn to a "different" gospel that presents "another" Jesus not portrayed in Scripture.* Be careful...this can happen to you too (2 Cor. 11:3-4).

- **It's the "Slow Cook" of the Frog.** Abrupt changes didn't deceive Judah...it was the gradual and progressive infusion of religious mixture (Zeph. 1:4-6). It's the slow-growing tares and the unnoticed perversion of God's grace that brings deception (Matt. 13:25; Jude 4). *Jump out of that simmering pot, my friend...before it's too late!*

How then does the book of Zephaniah help you Navigate your life? Consider this:

1. **If "Over-The-Top" Christians Really Do Annoy You, You May Be in Trouble and Don't Know it!** Pride makes a person look with disdain upon exuberant faith. Judah was destroyed because they lost their zeal for the Lord and His truth. *Better to be overly zealous and live than to die of apathy!*

2. **Learn the Lesson from Judah's Failure.** Tragically, the early Christians in Laodicea never learned those lessons. Read Rev. 3:14-22 to see how seriously Jesus views the lack of spiritual enthusiasm. *Live a balanced life; add wisdom to your zeal and zeal to your wisdom.*

3. **If You Realize You're Going Down the Same Path as Judah, Turn Back While You Still Have Time!** Whenever the Lord gives strong warnings, He also gives a way of escape. Return to

your first love, dear heart, and you will live (Rev. 2:4-7). Then, like God promised Judah, He will remove His judgments from you (Zeph. 3:14-20)!

What is God's Spirit Saying to Me...
As I Navigate Life According To Zephaniah

HAGGAI

God's Ultimate Solution When You Say... "I Can't Do This!"

Do you know people who have every excuse in the world for not doing what they know they should do? Guess what God says to them? *You may be surprised!*

- What does "I Can't" really mean?
- What problem did Israel have that could threaten your relationship with the Lord today?
- Five reasons why <u>GOD</u> says, "You Can" when <u>YOU</u> say, "I Can't!"

God's Ultimate Solution When You Say... "I Can't Do This!"

I can't get a job because _____. I can't achieve my potential because _____. I can't reach my teenager because _____. I can't do what God is asking me to do because _____. Have you ever heard yourself saying these things? *"I Can't"* means different things to different people. It could mean, *"I don't have the ability"*...or *"I'm not allowed to do this"*...or *"I'm afraid!"*...or *"I Won't!"* But in the days of Haggai, it meant, *"I'm too busy with my own life to worry about what God wants me to do!"*

Seventy years was a long time...long enough for Israel to grow apathetic toward God's priorities. That's how long they were held captive in Babylon. And why did the Lord send them there? Because they had forsaken Him and adopted the false religions of the land. When their seventy-year sentence was over, they had been cured of idolatry but they faced a new battle...***spiritual lethargy!*** The House of God lay in ruins and all they could think of was re-building comfortable homes and prosperous businesses. The old prophet, Haggai, didn't hold back when he chastised their lack of zeal for God. ***Like a divine defibrillator, he jolted lethargic hearts out of complacency into obedience.*** The people claimed they couldn't rebuild God's House because they lacked prosperity. God gave them a Divine Attitude Adjustment by informing them that their lack of prosperity was because of their lack of obedience (Hag. 1:1-11)! ***Then, with incredible love and grace, God gave them the Ultimate Solution to all human excuses...HIS PRESENCE! Twice the Lord declared, "I...AM...WITH...YOU!" (Hag. 1:13; 2:4-5).***

So, what does *"I Am With You"* really mean and how does this help you to Navigate your Life and Destiny? Consider this:

1. **"I Am With You"...*I Have Graciously Chosen to Forgive You of Your Sins.*** Sin separates fallen humanity from the Living God. The only way we can regain His presence and His blessings is to call upon the Lord with a repentant heart. When you trust in Jesus, God's Son, and what He did for you, He will restore your relationship with God and the Destiny to which you were called (Eph. 1:4-12).

2. **"I Am With You"...*You No Longer Have a Right to Be Afraid (Is. 41:10; Acts 18:10).*** Fear paralyzes obedience. But when you know the Lord is with you, you are free to obey Him knowing He will go before you, empower you, fight for you and protect you from all that is evil.

3. **"I Am With You"...*I Will Fulfill My Promises to You (Gen. 28:15).*** The question that many ask is, *"Will God really DO what He said He would do?"* God is not a man that He should lie (Num. 23:19)! God's presence confirms His intention to fulfill His promises to you (Heb. 6:13-19).

4. **"I Am With You"...*I Will Work With Your Children (Is. 43:5).*** The prayer of every godly parent is for their children to follow the Lord. God's presence means that He is helping you to be a righteous example for your children to follow. Then the Lord will do the rest (Prov. 22:6).

5. **"I Am With You"...*You Can Have Full Confidence of Success In Whatever I Send You To Do (Matt. 28:18-20).*** It's amazing how many Christians are afraid to share Christ with friends and family. When God is with you, it's not YOU that saves people...it's HIM! Speak with confidence and gentleness and watch the Lord as He draws people to Himself.

So, my friend, where are your excuses for not doing what the Lord has called you to do? God has taken all of them away by these simple words, *"I...AM...WITH...YOU!"*

What is God's Spirit Saying to Me...
As I Navigate Life According To Haggai

ZECHARIAH

Rebuilding a Destroyed Life Doing it God's Way!

What does God do with a ruined life? He reverses evil and restores it back to Himself again...IF the heart is right! *If you know someone who's in trouble, this teaching will help you minister to them.*

- What does the book of Zechariah have to do with rebuilding lives?
- Can anything good come out of a ruined life?
- Five essentials for rebuilding a life that's been destroyed.

Rebuilding a Destroyed Life
Doing it God's Way!

It was in total ruins...homes, businesses and the walls that surrounded the great city of Jerusalem. Even the House of God had been reduced to dust and rubble. The glorious Temple, once the site of sacred worship and joyous celebrations, had been desecrated and stripped of its treasures. That was the horrific scene the Israelites discovered as they returned from 70 years of captivity in Babylon. In spite of this, as with most resolute people, they immediately began the arduous task of rebuilding the world they once knew. However, the worst of the devastation that befell Israel wasn't the city or even the loss of human life. *It was their spiritual relationship with God that lay in ruins! Israel needed more than supplies and skilled workers to rebuild their lives...they needed spiritual reformation!*

Someone, right now, is reading this teaching wondering if it's even possible to rebuild their life again. Perhaps you've just returned from <u>Prison</u> and are trying to start over in a world of rejection. Maybe you're still reeling from a brutal <u>Divorce</u> wondering how your life will ever be the same again. Or it could be you've <u>Lost</u> a husband, wife or someone very dear to you and you feel you have nothing to live for anymore. Possibly, your <u>Job</u> was jerked out from underneath your feet and you're trying to rebuild your career. *If this describes you, then the book of Zechariah will give insight into how you can navigate the rebuilding of your life...God's Way.*

1. First Things First...Secure Your Relationship With The Lord. Most people in crisis mode put self-preservation first...food, shelter, safety, etc. Like Israel, they fail to realize that without God they may be able to survive physically, but they'll die spiritually. *When your world crashes down, you desperately need God's favor. That only happens when you put Him first (Zech. 1:3)!*

2. **Rebuild Your Place of Worship.** For Israel, it was Solomon's great Temple of God that needed to be rebuilt (Zech. 8:9-13). Yet Zechariah's message directed the people to a different kind of temple...the one that only Messiah could build (Zech. 6:12-13)! *You, my friend, are God's House...His dwelling place (Eph. 2:19-22). Rebuild it and He will meet you there!*

3. **Learn From Your Past.** Zechariah reminded the people that past failures were the cause of their captivity in Babylon (Zech. 1:2-6). Can anything good come out of the horrific experiences you've had to walk through? Absolutely Yes! *You can learn not to repeat mistakes; and God can use you to comfort others who are going through similar experiences (2 Cor. 1:3-4).*

4. **To Be Sure, You Will Always Have an Accuser Waiting to Sabotage Your Progress.** One of the most amazing accounts in scripture is **Zech. 3:1-7.** (Take a moment to read what happened.) With cunning and deceit, Satan blended facts and lies together to weave a garment of guilt and condemnation for Joshua the high priest. *When this happens, do what Joshua did...let God defend you! He can do it far better than you!*

5. Finally, **Step Into Your Restored Destiny.** After the Lord rebuked the accuser and cleansed Joshua the high priest, He placed him back into his calling again **(Zech. 3:6-7).** Regardless of how destructive your experiences are, God wants to put you back where you belong...into your divine Destiny. *A life that trusts the Lord with a heart of humility is never destroyed! You'll never fail as long as you don't give up! That's God's way of rebuilding your life.*

Now you have it...your "Map" and your "Compass" by which you can navigate a path out of a ruined life and into God's Destiny. Hold them close to you at all times. *There's no Navigational Instruments like these...anywhere in the world!*

What is God's Spirit Saying to Me...
As I Navigate Life According To Zechariah

MALACHI

What Went Wrong?
Postmortem of a Broken Religious System

Some people believe it doesn't matter what they believe. In fact, Israel mixed all beliefs together into a religious cocktail thinking they all lead to God. ***Guess what God thought about that?***

- Why did Israel's Religious System self-destruct?
- What are the progressive warning signs that they ignored?
- How can you prevent this from happening to you?

What Went Wrong?
Postmortem of a Broken Religious System

"What Went Wrong?!" That's what everybody demands to know when tragedy strikes. It's when a routine medical procedure ends in death; an aircraft falls out of the sky and kills hundreds; and a seemingly peaceful man goes berserk and sprays bullets into his former place of employment. When these horror stories occur, teams of specialists are brought in to try to piece together the fragments of evidence. They're trying to determine "What Went Wrong." They're trying to learn how to prevent the unthinkable from happening again. *So what happens when a Religious System self-destructs? God sends in His specialists...His prophets! They speak, not out of their own human opinions, but from the very heart of God to declare "What Went Wrong."* Such was the task of Malachi.

What was it like to live in the days of Malachi? **The priests polluted their offerings, profaned the Covenant, encouraged apostasy, twisted the Word of God to teach falsely and robbed God by misusing the tithe. In short, they destroyed the precious belief system that God had charged them to guard.** So hopeless and irreversible was their apostasy that *God **dismantled** their broken religious system, wiped the slate clean and started all over again.* That's why Malachi is the final book in the Old Testament. The next book you read in the Christian Bible begins with Jesus...God's Son who came to the earth and declared, *"I will build **MY** church"* (Matt. 16:18). The old broken system had passed away and God began with a New Covenant and a New High Priest...Jesus, God's faithful Son (Heb. 8:6-13). He fulfilled ALL the Law with <u>His Works</u>, not the futile attempts of Adam's fallen race.

So, What Went Wrong? Could it be that you and I are in danger of repeating the failures of Israel? Not if we take heed to the progressive warning signs that come from Malachi's Postmortem investigation.

1. **SPIRITUAL DULLNESS** (Malachi 1). Israel's leaders were dying and didn't know it! They were oblivious to their actions that displeased God and were totally unaware that they had failed to honor God. *Spiritual Dullness never happens quickly...it slowly develops over years of closing your ears to the voice of God speaking through His Word and True Leadership.*

2. Spiritual Dullness Leads to **TOXIC RELATIONSHIPS** (Malachi 2). The Jews were divorcing their wives to marry pagan women. The issue wasn't racial...it was spiritual! Interfaith marriage is the mingling of souls and spirits! *Guard yourself from the slow-acting poison of spiritual mixture!*

3. Toxic Relationships Lead to **WITHHOLDING FROM GOD** (Malachi 3). Wrong influences change priorities. The first of the Ten Commandments reads, *"You shall have no other gods before Me!"* *Tithes and Offerings are not about money...they're about what's FIRST in your life!*

4. Withholding From God Leads to **REJECTING GOD'S COVENANT** (Malachi 4). Israel had forgotten (rejected) the Covenant God made with them through Moses. Yet God gave them the glorious promise of Restoration through a New Covenant. *Woe to us if we ever slip away from God's New Covenant in Jesus. There are no other ways to God. It's the final offer from God for Redemption and Eternal Life.*

Malachi's Postmortem pieced together the fragmented evidence of a Broken Religious System. Learn the lessons well, my friend. Our only hope for Eternal Life is the New Covenant based on faith in God's Son. *Don't allow spiritual mixture to exist in your life and don't follow the pattern of Israel (Isaiah 48:18-19)! Instead, follow the Compass of God's Sprit as He leads you in His Everlasting Way.*

What is God's Spirit Saying to Me...
As I Navigate Life According To Malachi

MATTHEW

Four Myths About Messiah
Many Christians Still Believe Them Today!

When God's Son, the Promised Messiah, stepped onto the world scene, the religious community who was waiting for Him couldn't recognize who He was. Why? *They had conjured up myths...just like many of us do today!*

- What were the myths the Jews believed about the coming Messiah?

- What are the myths that Christians today may believe about Jesus?

- What was Jesus' answer when He was asked if He was the Messiah?

Four Myths About Messiah
Many Christians Still Believe Them Today!

Fact or Fiction? That's the question the **Myth Busters** television series began asking in 2003. Their aim was to uncover the truth behind popular myths and legends by using scientific experiments. *Actually it's quite a fascinating program...if you have that kind of curiosity.* Here are some of the "world-shaking" questions the team put to rest:

- Can combining Diet Coke and Mentos make your stomach explode?
- Can plugging your finger in a gun barrel cause it to backfire?
- Can giant alligators really live in sewers?
- Could roaches really survive a nuclear explosion?

Well, here's a question from John the Baptist that might stump the Myth Busters team. While still in prison, John heard of the works of Christ (the Messiah) and sent word by his disciples asking, *"Are You the Expected One, or shall we look for someone else?"* (Matt. 11:2-3). In other words, the religious community had certain perceptions of who Messiah would be and what He would do. For 4,000 years after Adam and Eve's spiritual failure in the Garden of Eden, humankind had been looking for the "Seed of the woman" who would "crush the head" of the serpent (Gen. 3:15). Across the millenniums, their views shifted from divine reality to self-centered humanism. *Therefore, when Messiah really did show up, they couldn't recognize Him. Two thousand years later, many Christians still have misconceptions about who Jesus really is and what He does.*

Question: Is it possible that you and I have bought into some beliefs that are actually Myths? **Answer:** YES! Here are four of them:

1. **Jesus Will Deliver Me From ALL My Problems.** The Jewish concept of Messiah was that He would be the "Anointed One" sent by God to deliver them from oppressive situations in life. Unfortunately we can adopt that view as well. Then when bad things happen, it's easy to blame God for not stopping it. *Jesus came to restore our Relationship with God...not to solve all our natural problems in life.*

2. **Since Jesus Is "The Conqueror," He Will Overthrow All My Enemies.** The Jews were constantly being conquered. So, they saw Messiah as a Military Conqueror who would overthrow the oppression of Rome. We do too! Some Christians expect God to win their court cases and remove overbearing bosses. *Jesus conquered the Power of Sin and the Devil for those who trust in Him. But He expects us to handle our human conflict issues with godly wisdom! (Rom. 12:17-21; 1 Pet. 3:8-9)*

3. **Jesus Will Make Me a "King" in the Marketplace...I'll Be Rich!** Somehow the Jews felt that because God loved them, He would establish Israel as the preeminent political power in the world. Wrong! If we're not careful, we Christians can get the idea that our Savior will make us financially wealthy, just because He loves us! *Jesus gives us the Spiritual Wealth of Heaven, not opulent splendor on earth!*

4. **I'll Ride in With Jesus on a White Horse to Slay the Wicked!** To the Jews, Messiah was a Warrior King in flashing armor. So when Jesus rode into Jerusalem as a humble servant, coming in love and riding on a donkey, they rejected Him. *Sooner or later, we have to realize that Jesus is the Lord of Love. He wants to rescue the wicked, not slay them! That's our assignment as well.*

So, what was Jesus' answer when John asked if He was the One? *"Go and report to John what you hear and see: the blind receive sight and the lame walk, the lepers are cleansed and the deaf hear, the dead are raised up, and the poor have the gospel preached to them. And blessed is he who does not take offense at Me." (Matt. 11:4-6).* **Jesus came to open deaf ears and blinded eyes as to who God really is. He healed our spiritual walk and cleansed our sins. He gave us the "Good News" that heaven is open to those who trust in Him.** That's not a myth, my friend. THAT'S WHO MESSIAH REALLY IS!

What is God's Spirit Saying to Me...
As I Navigate Life According To Matthew

MARK

Two Famous "Losers" You'll Never Guess What They Did for God!

If you've ever attended Sunday school or church, you've heard about the Gospel According to Mark. ***But here's what you don't know...it was written by two people who the world would call "Losers!"***

- What do you mean "two" people? I thought Mark wrote this by himself?
- Why would God use "losers?"
- Nice story. But how can this help me navigate my life?

Two Famous "Losers"
You'll Never Guess What They Did for God!

Ever felt like you were a First Class Loser? You know what I mean...like a person who failed miserably just when others depended upon you the most. You disappointed yourself, your friends and even God! It might have been a financial failure, a family failure, a moral failure or a spiritual failure. But regardless of how it happened, the end result is the same...you were branded as a LOSER! You were scorned, ridiculed and rejected! But worst of all, you lost trust in yourself and wanted to run away and hide as fast as you could. *Now, what if I told you the first written Gospel of Jesus Christ was authored, not by a man of sterling character, but by TWO "LOSERS" who worked together...Mark and Peter!*

Okay, before you get offended, let me explain the rest of the story. Mark was a zealous young man who wanted to save the world. He joined the Apostle Paul and Barnabas, his cousin, as they embarked on their first missionary journey to Asia Minor. Guess what happened? *Mark either got offended or he couldn't handle the hardships and "chickened out"! Whatever the reason, he deserted them and returned to Jerusalem (Acts 13:5, 13).* Paul thought he was such a "loser" that he rejected him and vehemently refused to take him on their next mission (Acts 15:36-40). Whatever happened to Mark? *Barnabas encouraged him and, according to many Bible scholars, Mark wrote the first account of Jesus' life...even before Matthew. It's called "The Gospel According to Mark."*

And then there was Peter...you know his story. *He brashly declared his undying commitment to Jesus (Mark 14:29-31) and then later, because of fear, he flatly denied ever knowing Him (Mark 14:66-72).* It's amazing how Mark knew the details of Peter's failure. According to Bible scholars, Peter was close to Mark's family (Acts 12:11-12) and Mark probably was a convert of Peter (1 Pet. 5:13). They believe

Mark's descriptive accounts of Jesus' life came from Peter, himself, who was one of Jesus' closest disciples. Some commentators have said that Mark's Gospel could have easily been called, "Peter's Gospel." *Yet, in spite of Peter's one-time cowardly act, God saw greatness in Peter's heart. It was he who the Holy Spirit anointed to boldly stand up and prophesy on the Day of Pentecost (Acts 2:14-41).*

How then does knowing who wrote the Gospel of Mark help you navigate your Destiny? Consider this:

1. **Your Flesh Can Betray Who You <u>REALLY</u> Are.** All of us do things in life that we're not proud of. Our fallen nature (our flesh) can get the best of us and we can let down the people we love the most. *Like Mark and Peter, you are greater than your failures. God created you for greatness. Trust the Lord, repent and move forward into the purpose for which you were destined.*

2. **<u>GOD</u> Is Greater Than Your Failures (1 John 3:20).** Regardless of how condemning your failures might be, God can remove your transgression against Him. Why? *Because He loves you and has deep compassion for your plight in life (Ps. 103:8-14). Believe God more than your heart or your failures.*

3. **With God, the End of a Matter Is Better Than the Beginning (Eccles. 7:8).** When you come to God with a humble heart, He can reverse your failures and give you a better life than before. *Like Mark and Peter, you'll be amazed at the people the Lord can influence through you.*

4. **You're Never a "Loser" if God is With You.** God's Son came to the earth for this very reason...to redeem people who have <u>Lost Out</u> with God. When you place your faith in Jesus, you are washed, sanctified and justified. *If God is for you, who can be against you (Rom. 8:31)!*

What is God's Spirit Saying to Me...
As I Navigate Life According To Mark

LUKE

Jesus in 4-D and High-Definition
What You'd Miss if You Didn't Read Luke

Do you know anyone who lives in a "two-dimensional" world? They're missing out on the depth of what life is all about. ***Likewise, without FOUR Gospels your Faith will be deficient!***

- What do you mean, "Jesus In 4-D and High-Definition?"
- What would I miss if I didn't read Luke's Gospel?
- How does this help me to navigate my life?

Jesus in 4-D and High-Definition
What You'd Miss if You Didn't Read Luke

"Two-Dimensional" means that an image has width and height. In other words, it's FLAT. "Three-Dimensional" (3-D) means an additional dimension has been added...it has DEPTH. You can see the complete view or concept of an object with profound quality and insight. Actually, that's why God gave us two eyes...to give us depth perception. Our eyes see the same object from two slightly different angles. In an amazing bio-engineering marvel, God created the brain to blend the views from both eyes to see objects with Three-Dimensional Depth. That's also why God gave us ***FOUR slightly different accounts of Jesus' life***...one from **Matthew's** perspective; another from **Mark**; a third from **Luke** and a fourth from **John**. *Now you have what I call "Jesus in 4-D"...Four Gospels that give profound insight into what God is really like and how he expects you to live (Heb. 1:1-4).*

So, what would happen if you didn't read Luke's account of the life of Jesus? *Well, for starters, more than half of the material in Luke (much of 9:51-19:27) is found in no other Gospel.* Here are some essential pieces of your faith that would be missing:

1. You Wouldn't Know How To Deal With People Who REJECT You (Luke 9:51-56).

2. You Wouldn't Know the Story of the Good Samaritan and What "LOVE Your NEIGHBOR" Really Means (Luke 10:25-37).

3. You Wouldn't Know That You're Supposed To PRAY With PERSISTENCE (Luke 11:5-8).

4. You Wouldn't Know What to Think About <u>NATURAL DISASTERS</u> and <u>BRUTAL MASSACRES</u> (Luke 13:1-5).

5. You Wouldn't Know The Story of The Prodigal Son and How Much God <u>LOVES and WAITS For SINNERS</u> To Return To Him (Luke 15:11-32).

6. You Wouldn't Know The Story of Lazarus and The Rich Man and About God's <u>JUSTICE</u> In The Afterlife (Luke 16:19-31).

7. You Wouldn't Know The Story of Zaccheus and How Much Jesus <u>LOVES People That You HATE</u> (Luke 19:1-10)!

So, how does all of this help you to navigate your life and destiny in Christ?

1. **Get a 4-D and a High-Definition View of Jesus.** That means when you read all Four Gospels, you get four times the clarity and detail of who Jesus really is and how He expects you to live.

2. **Don't Settle for a "Two-Dimensional" Life.** There are many dimensions to life: Physical, Emotional, Spiritual, Work, Rest, Family, Friends and Church-life. If you leave any of them out, you'll have a deficient view of life.

3. **View People and Situations From All Angles.** This gives you Depth Perception. If you don't do this, you'll misunderstand, misjudge and miss what God is teaching you through them.

The "Map" of the Gospels is absolutely essential to your Christian Faith and maturity in Christ. Without it you'll never know how much God loves you. Without it you'll never know the true character of God as revealed in His Son, Jesus. Once you have that Map, then the "Compass" of God's Spirit will point the way to full Redemption and

Eternal Life. When you follow God's Map and Compass, you'll surely discover and arrive at your divine Destiny in Him.

What is God's Spirit Saying to Me...
As I Navigate Life According To Luke

JOHN

Last Man Standing!
How the Last Living Apostle Described Jesus

You don't want to know what life was _really_ like for Christians after Jesus' resurrection. It was a killing field! Yet one man survived the holocaust to tell his story. **You need to hear what he had to say!**

- Who did John say that Jesus really is?
- What is the Christian Faith all about?
- What happens if you extract John's description of Jesus from your faith?

Last Man Standing!
How the Last Living Apostle Described Jesus

If you're a Bruce Willis fan, you couldn't forget his 1996 movie, "Last Man Standing." He's the "good" bad-guy who does kind deeds while he's killing everybody! When the dust clears, he's the only one left alive in a gang shoot-out. *Sure, it was pretty violent...but so is the real world!*

The Apostle John was also the "Last Man Standing"...but he really WAS a "Good Guy." The world he lived in was violent beyond your imagination. Christians were on a "short list" of people scheduled for total eradication by a power-crazed maniac Roman Emperor named Nero. Christians were being thrown to lions for sport and burned alive as human torches to light Nero's garden. All of John's fellow apostles that he had walked with had been martyred...crucified, beheaded or beaten to death. John suffered extreme persecution and was exiled to the penal colony on the island called Patmos. It was there, on that hellish island, that God transported him into the heavenly realm to see what no man has ever seen before. It was there that he recorded the conclusion to our Christian Bible...The "Revelation" of Jesus Christ! *According to tradition, he later lived out his life in Ephesus after returning from Patmos. Amazingly, he died of natural causes in his 90's...sixty-eight years after our Lord's Resurrection.*

Having outlived all the apostles who personally knew and walked with Jesus, John's testimony becomes even more impelling. How then did this "Last Apostle Standing" see and describe Jesus?

1. Jesus Is *GOD* (John 1:1-2, 34). No other Gospel writer was more crystal clear about this than John. Jesus wasn't just another great prophet, a wonderful healer or a miracle worker. *He was the "Living Word"...the Second Person of the Godhead who existed before time began!*

2. Jesus Is The *__CREATOR__* (John 1:3). Jesus wasn't just a bystander with God...He was God who created the heavens and the earth (Col. 1:16-17)! Now you see why Jesus could so easily perform miracles. *That's also why He could give His authority to believers to do the same (Matt. 10:1).*

3. Jesus Is The *__INCARNATE GOD__* (John 1:14-18). The Son of God came to the earth, became flesh and lived as a real human being with people. His "human name" was Jesus...meaning "God is Salvation." Why did He do this? *So that we would know what God is really like (John 1:18; Heb. 1:3). People were lost in the darkness of sin (John 1:4-10; Matt. 4:16) and didn't have a clue how to be redeemed back to God again (John 3:3-8, 36; Acts 4:12).*

4. Your Salvation Depends On How You *__PERSONALLY RESPOND__* To Jesus (John 1:12; 3:15-21). No, my friends. Salvation is NOT an "automatic" result of Jesus' work on Calvary's Cross and His Resurrection. *If you don't personally TRUST in what He did for you...you're LOST (Mark 16:16)!*

5. Jesus Is Not Only "God, The Savior"...He's "God, The *__JUDGE__* of The World!" (Rev. 1:8-18) Most people don't want to see Jesus like this. But it's true whether you believe it or not! Even as John saw Jesus **before** time began, his final description of Jesus was at the **end** of time. Don't think for a moment that God will not judge evil people at the end of the world (Rev. 20:10-15). *But you don't have to fear this judgment...if you personally believe in Jesus (John 5:21-27).*

And that's the "Map" that John left us in his Gospel. Your belief system as a Christian is all about Jesus, what He did for you and how you must personally respond to Him! *Christianity isn't Christianity if you take Jesus out of the equation or twist the Bible to make Him less than who John and the other Gospel writers and Paul said He is. No person or other belief systems can give you Eternal Life but Jesus. Believe in Him and you will have the Life of God living in you (Acts 16:31)!* Then when you follow the "Compass" of God's Spirit, He will lead you into a deeper and even more personal **relationship** with God through His Son, Jesus (John 16:13-15).

What is God's Spirit Saying to Me...
As I Navigate Life According To John

ACTS

How Healthy Is Your Church?
Take This Test and Find Out!

Have you ever wondered why some churches are "alive" and others aren't? *The book of Acts holds the answer to your question and gives you the key to a "Healthy" Church.*

- How can I tell if my church is healthy or sick?
- What does a healthy church look like?
- But won't this test make me critical or judgmental?

How Healthy Is Your Church?
Take This Test and Find Out!

Why is the church down the street "alive" and "growing"...but mine isn't? Why are some churches vibrant hubs of God's energy while others are stale and lifeless? These are questions that many people (and some pastors) are asking. But they can't figure out the answer. Unfortunately, the problems of unhealthy churches are very complex, numerous and far beyond the scope of this short article. However, there are some very similar analogies between a "sick" church and a "sick" human body. Perhaps the question that should be asked is... *"What does a 'Healthy' church look like?"*

The book of Acts is the story of the birth and growth of the Christian Church in the world. It was written by Luke as he traveled with the Apostle Paul in his journeys. Interestingly, Luke was a physician (Col. 4:14) who was trained to help sick people become healthy. As the book of Acts begins, we discover the anatomy of Jesus' church...what He intended it to be and how it is supposed to function. ***The following is a "Church Health Questionnaire" I've developed from Acts 2:40-47. Take this test and see how healthy your church is.***

1. Are You Reaching the <u>Lost</u>? *(Acts 2:40-41)*. The primary mission of the Church is to be witnesses of Christ throughout the earth (Acts. 1:8). If this isn't happening, you have no life!

2. Are You Eating the Right <u>Food</u>? *(Acts 2:42)*. The "Apostles Doctrine" became our New Testament. If you're not continually devoted to God's written word...you'll slowly die!

3. Are You <u>Partaking</u> of the Lord? *(Acts 2:42)*. "Breaking of Bread" is not just bread and wine; it's the intimate presence of Christ with one another at the Communion Table. That's true Life!

4. Are You <u>Praying</u> Together? *(Acts 2:42)*. Something deeply spiritual happens when you pray together as believers. Prayer isn't a monologue...it's a dialogue! Are you listening for His voice while you're praying?

5. Do You Have a Sense of <u>Expectation</u>? *(Acts 2:43)*. Sunday mornings should never be just a "religious" obligation. If you're not expecting God's awesome presence, you have no zeal!

6. Is God's <u>Supernatural Power</u> Actively at Work? *(Acts 2:43)*. If God's power is not miraculously healing, delivering and setting people free from bondages, your ministry is powerless.

7. Do You Have "Contagious" <u>Love and Generosity</u>? *(Acts 2:44-45)*. A community of love is not just being aware of human needs...it sacrificially meets those needs. That kind of love is contagious!

8. Are You In "<u>Concert</u>" With One Another? *(Acts 2:46)*. In a healthy church, its members blend their gifts and callings together to form a Holy Spirit symphony for the world to see (John 17:21).

9. Is Your <u>Church Experience</u> More Than Just Sunday Mornings? *(Acts 2:46)*. Unless you're meeting in home groups and fellowshipping around meals, Christianity becomes institutional.

10. Is the <u>Lord</u> Drawing People to You? *(Acts 2:47)*. When the Lord is at work in His Church, the word gets around. Remember, people are drawn to God...not to fancy buildings!

Now, after evaluating your church, here's what you should discover. This test is actually for <u>YOU</u>! Why? Because <u>YOU</u> are God's Church, His "Called-Out-Ones," whom He redeemed and sends into the world to represent the Savior (Acts 1:8). *Now, retake this test and make it personal. If we all do our parts, even a sick church can become healthy...if we become healthy. Try it and see!*

What is God's Spirit Saying to Me...
As I Navigate Life According To Acts

ROMANS

This Book Changed Christianity Forever
It Can Transform You Too!

Do you know Christians who are struggling with sin...fearing God's judgment and punishment? They're not alone! *That's one reason why God stirred Paul's heart to write the Book of Romans.*

- Guess what famous person also struggled with personal sin?
- What did he do that changed Christianity forever?
- How does what he discovered help you live in spiritual peace?

This Book Changed Christianity Forever
It Can Transform You Too!

Day after day he struggled with God over his sins. Though he had committed his very soul to the Savior, he failed to line up his life with God's Laws and requirements for righteous living. And for that failure, he knew he would face divine judgment and punishment. So, what was the solution his church offered him? His sins could be pardoned and God's punishment removed...for a <u>FEE</u>! *But when more sins were committed, the "Forgiveness for a Fee" ritual was repeated...for as long as he lived!*

And that was the way of Christianity for 400 years. This practice began in 1100 A.D. when Pope Urban II remitted all penance of persons who participated in the Crusades and who confessed their sins. Later, the indulgences were also offered to those who couldn't go on the Crusades but offered <u>Cash Contributions</u> to the effort instead. By 1200 A.D. the church began claiming that it had a "Treasury" of Indulgences (consisting of the merits of Christ <u>AND</u> the Saints) that it could dispense in ways that "promoted" the church and its mission. In 1517, Pope Leo X needed funds to complete the building of St. Peter's Basilica in Rome. For that reason, he entered into an arrangement that sold indulgence franchises—half could be retained by local churches and the other half for Leo's construction project. Thus the sinful soul was promised an escape from purgatory...*until one man read Rom.1:17 "<u>The righteous man shall live by faith</u>" and Rom. 5:1 "Having been <u>justified by faith</u>, we have <u>peace with God</u> through our Lord Jesus Christ."* Who was that man who struggled over his damnable sins? *He was Martin Luther, a Roman Monk! It was he who wrote the 95 Theses against the abuses of the clergy. It was he who began the Christian Reformation in the year 1517 that changed Christianity forever.*

Navigating Life With God's Compass

So, what does all this mean for you and me who have faith in Jesus for our eternal salvation? In other words...How can you navigate your life according to the "Map" of Romans?

1. **It Frees You From Trying To "Earn" Righteousness.** When Paul wrote his letter to the Roman Christians, he knew they struggled to live righteously in a pagan world. Some were being drawn back into old lifestyles while others were anguishing over their sins as did Martin Luther. And so are we...nearly 500 years later! *Both Paul and Martin Luther taught that neither YOU nor a church can "Do" anything to sidestep your sin or its consequences. Jesus already did that for you!*

2. **Does That Mean I Can Live Anyway I Want?** The fallen nature is quite creative. If Christians are made "Righteous" by Christ's work and not their own, then perhaps there's no use in even TRYING to live righteously! Paul clearly addressed this misconception in Rom. 5:20-6:23. "Religion" says you can only be righteous by your conduct. *Christianity says you are righteous by your FAITH in Christ...and THAT causes you to discipline yourself to live righteously!*

Finally, here's a difficult question that must be asked: Do the problems that Martin Luther encountered continue in the church today? My answer is, *"I certainly hope not!"* However...

1. If you think you can do enough good deeds to offset the bad stuff you've done in life...*then you're falling into error.* Only Jesus has the solution for sin that gives you eternal life!

2. If you give tithes and offerings in order to influence God to remove the debt you brought upon yourself...*you're wrong!* We give because we love God...not to make God do something for us!

3. If someone tells you God will bless <u>YOU</u> more than your neighbor if you give large sums of money to the church's building fund...*be careful!* That's too close to what happened in 1517!

I encourage you, my friend, to read Romans. Like Martin Luther, it'll transform your life forever!

What is God's Spirit Saying to Me...
As I Navigate Life According To Romans

1 CORINTHIANS

The Most Scandalous Church on the Planet! Who Are They?

Think your church has problems? You don't KNOW what problems are until you read about this totally dysfunctional church. *They're worse than you can possibly imagine!*

- Who is this church and what did they do?
- What did God do to them?
- Knowing these things, how then shall you live your life?

The Most Scandalous Church on the Planet! Who Are They?

Disgusting, factious and openly immoral! Pompous, carnal and immature! Insolent, selfish and fleshly! That might be the way a visitor would describe this church. In fact, when their general overseer heard of their carnality, he called them *"fornicators, idolaters, adulterers, homosexuals, thieves, covetous, drunkards, revilers, and swindlers!"* Then he took it a step further and proclaimed that people like this, *"Will not inherit the Kingdom of God!"* Okay...so who are these dysfunctional Christians and where is their church? No, it's not the church down the street or the church you just left. And it's not the church where you are now. **It was the great church in Corinth that the Apostle Paul founded in 50 AD!**

Sooner or later we all have to come to the sad realization that there are NO "perfect" churches and NO "perfect" Christians. Now, here's another tragic discovery you'll make...you've probably done some of the same things the Christians in Corinth did! So, what did God do to the scandalous and dysfunctional people at Corinth? **He RESCUED them!** Listen to God's unbelievable mercy and grace in the Apostle Paul's writings, *"And such were some of you! But you were washed, but you were sanctified, but you were justified in the name of the Lord Jesus." (1 Cor. 6:9-11).* If you ask for forgiveness, repent and trust in Jesus, He can do the same for you too.

Now that you've been introduced to "The Most Scandalous Church on the Planet" and what God did for them, how does this help you to navigate your life? Consider this:

1. **Guard Yourself Against "World Poisoning!"** The world can slip into your life before you know it. Like the Corinthian church, the spirit of the world can poison your soul. So, what's God's antidote for world poisoning? It's called the Cross! The

Cross is foolishness for those who rely on the flesh, ***but for Christians it's the power of salvation!*** (1 Cor. 1:18; 2:12; 1 John 2:15-17).

2. **Learn the Difference Between Separation and Influence.** If you read 2 Cor. 6:14-17, you'd conclude the Bible requires total separation from the world. But in 1 Cor. 5:9-13 and John 17:14-18 you read that unless you associate with the world, you can't influence them for Christ. So it's all about "who's influencing who!" ***Make sure the world isn't influencing you!***

3. **So, What'cha Gonna' Do With All Those Sinners in Your Church?** Before you judge others, take a close look at your own life. Since you were once like them, what did God do with you? *"But,"* you may ask, *"What about people who continue to act like the world?"* Ask yourself, *"How does God deal with **me** when **I** continue to sin?"* ***His love gently draws us to repentance!***

4. **Learn How To Escape Temptation.** Sin disguises itself as justifiable actions...sins we enjoy but don't want to release. Some believe that because they belong to Christ, they can act any way they want. Yet in each case, God sends warnings (1 Cor. 10:13). It may be a sermon, a talk with a friend or a quiet whisper in your heart. ***Take heed, my friend. It may mean life or death!***

5. **Jesus Forgives, But Don't Take Sin Lightly...It Can Disqualify You!** As spiritually secure as Paul was, he wrote, *"I discipline my body and make it my slave, so that, after I have preached to others, I myself will not be disqualified"* (1 Cor. 9:27). Sin destroys your witness and your ministry. And it causes young Christians to stumble (Matt. 18:6-7). ***But when you repent and embrace the Savior, He welcomes you back to where you belong!*** Just read Luke 15:11-32 to see the Father's love, grace and mercy toward you!

What is God's Spirit Saying to Me...
As I Navigate Life According To 1 Corinthians

2 CORINTHIANS

The Marks of a True Calling of God
It May Surprise You!

If you were ever challenged to prove that you really <u>ARE</u> who you <u>SAY</u> you are in ministry, how would you respond? Paul was put in this very position. *You may be surprised to learn how he validated his apostleship!*

- What validations do most of us give?
- Why was Paul put on the spot?
- Four proofs that Paul gave of his calling...you need to know these!

The Marks of a True Calling of God
It May Surprise You!

Do you have a genuine call of God on your life? If you do, how would you prove it? Some may answer, *"The Lord moved upon my heart and called me to serve Him."* Others may say, *"It's the lives that have been changed by my ministry."* Still others might proclaim, *"It's the supernatural power of God flowing through my life."* All of these are valid evidences of God's call. **But that's not how the Apostle Paul proved to the Corinthian church that he was a genuine Apostle of God.** You might be surprised to learn how Paul validated his calling.

Paul's <u>first</u> letter to the church he planted in Corinth was strong and corrective. There was mixture in the house, strife among people and a misunderstanding of what true spirituality really meant. As an Apostle of Christ, his assignment was to set the church in order with sound doctrine and godly practices. **But after receiving his painful letter, some didn't like it! In fact, they began to doubt his divine authority. And others questioned if he was even an Apostle at all!** Thus, when Paul wrote his <u>second</u> letter, he squarely addressed his accusers (2 Cor. 13:2-3). How would you defend yourself if this had been you? Listen carefully.

1. A Genuine Call of God Is a <u>Selfless</u> Life Lived Vicariously for Others (2 Cor. 4:5-10). When Paul defended his apostleship, he wrote, *"We do not preach ourselves but Christ Jesus as Lord, and ourselves as your bond-servants for Jesus' sake."* In other words, it's not about <u>US</u>...it's about <u>JESUS</u> and what <u>HE</u> did for people. *So, who are we who preach the Gospel? Just "jars of clay," inexpensive and easily broken, through whom the light of Jesus shines for <u>your</u> benefit.*

2. A True Call of God Includes Both <u>Glory</u> and <u>Dishonor</u> (2 Cor. 6:4-10). Ministry is a mixed bag. At times people honored

Paul and at other times they maligned and insulted him. At times he was commended and at other times condemned. Don't think honor alone is a mark of God's calling. If you are truly called, you will probably offend the self-righteous and judgmental. *Just be sure you're suffering for Christ, and not your own foolishness (1 Pet. 3:15-17)!*

3. A Genuine Call of God Is Accompanied by <u>Pain</u>, <u>Suffering</u> and <u>Hardships</u> (2 Cor. 11:22-28). A young seminary student wouldn't want to hear this, but it's true. As Paul continued his defense, he opened his life for others to see the true work of an apostle. It's not sitting in comfortable quarters writing letters to churches. Listen to Paul's qualifications: *"Imprisonments, beaten times without number, often in danger of death. Five times I received from the Jews thirty-nine lashes. Three times I was beaten with rods; once I was stoned; three times I was shipwrecked, a night and a day I have spent in the deep." Now...who wants to be an Apostle?*

4. A True Call of God Is Validated by God's <u>Revelatory</u> <u>Truth</u> (2 Cor. 12:1-4). Revelation is the self-disclosure of God concerning Himself and His eternal purposes for heaven and earth. Paul's mind had been opened to see the inner workings of God's Kingdom and His intentions for His Church. Paul saw through the veneer of human pride and arrogance. And he revealed the grace and patience of the Lord toward sinners. In short, Paul's assignment was to mature the Church to become the Bride of Christ. *But before you ask for this kind of encounter with God...read 2 Cor. 12:7. It comes with thorns!*

That, my friend, is how the Apostle Paul validated his call from God. So how do <u>YOU</u> measure up? Very few of us would be able to say, *"Oh sure...that's me!"* But what this does is make us deeply appreciate and honor the sacrificial work of men and women who have true callings from the Lord. Here's one more thing that Paul's example does. It humbles those of us who wear titles such as: Apostle, Prophet,

Evangelist, Pastor and Teacher. As Paul wrote, if you're going to boast, boast in your <u>weakness</u> and in God's <u>strength</u>! *"For when I am weak, then I am strong" (2 Cor. 12:9-10).*

What is God's Spirit Saying to Me...
As I Navigate Life According To 2 Corinthians

GALATIANS

Slipping Back to the Old Ways Again? Want a No-Guilt Solution?

Even people who love Jesus and trust in His saving grace still find themselves slipping back into the old patterns of life that He rescued them from. ***God wants to give us a Guilt-Free way to get back to Him.***

- Why do people still fight a losing battle against sin?
- What's the real problem that escapes their view?
- Four solutions when you find yourself slipping back into your old ways again.

Slipping Back to the Old Ways Again? Want a No-Guilt Solution?

The year was 1944. He was Lt. Hiroo Onoda of the Japanese Imperial Army. Sent to a remote Philippine island of Lubang, he was charged to conduct guerrilla warfare during World War II. But when the war ended a year later, he **NEVER GOT THE WORD!** For <u>29 years</u> he hid in the jungle fighting for his beloved Japan. And so it is with many Christians. We find ourselves fighting a senseless war that's over. Yet we hide out in the jungles of our minds struggling against our sinful natures, not understanding that Jesus already fought that war and won it! The Lt. Onoda story was so moving that it inspired Bill and Gloria Gaither to write their epic song, **"It Is Finished!"** *"Yet in my heart, the battle was still raging. Not all prisoners of war had come home. These were battlefields of my own making. I didn't know that the war had been won. Oh, but then I heard the King of the ages had fought all the battles for me; And that victory was mine for the claiming; And now praise his name, I am free!"*

The spiritual walk of many Christians is a guilty struggle against sin. They try to act righteous knowing that it's a losing battle! For the Galatian churches, their struggle was slipping back into legalism trying to keep an external set of Laws to remove the guilt of sin. They forgot that Jesus not only kept the Law for them, but He took their punishment, **removed their guilt** and forgave those who trust in His redemptive work! For many of us, our struggle is slipping back to worldly behavior. Here's the problem...**we forget who we are and what Jesus did for us!** When we're born again we're not the same person we used to be. Yet we act like we're still a slave to sin when we've been set free! Like the Japanese soldier, some **NEVER GET THE WORD!** Want God's guilt-free solution to your problem? Consider this:

1. **Umm...Maybe You Didn't Get The Memo? The Sinful Part of You Died at the Cross and You Don't Realize It (Gal. 2:20)!**

I know this is hard to understand, but it's true. As a Christian, you have to continually remind yourself that your fallen nature was "crucified with Christ" and you walk in "newness of life" (Rom. 6:4-7). *The degree to which you do this is the degree to which you really are FREE!*

2. News Flash...You're a SON, Not a Slave (Gal. 4:6-9)! That changes everything. When an upstanding family adopts a child, it means he/she has a New Beginning. The child previously born to unfit parents now has proper role models to shape his character. And so it is with you. Born into sin, you were a slave to the dictates of your fallen nature. *But now you have a New Father who gives you righteous "DNA." No longer a slave...you are His son (Rom. 8:14-15)!*

3. Yes, You're Free...But Not The Way You Think (Gal. 5:1, 13). "Freedom" means that you are no longer forced to live in sin. You are freed from the chains that keep you from righteous living. Yet, some interpret freedom as a license to sin. They enjoy their sins too much to be set free from them! *You can't fool God! Don't use your freedom as "an opportunity for the flesh."*

4. Follow Your New GPS..."God's Positioning System" (Gal. 5:16-25). When you're "off course" with God and have slipped back to your old ways again, God doesn't just leave you there. He guides you back on course with Him. God's Navigational GPS is His Spirit. The first thing He does is lead you to **REPENTANCE!** That means: **Stop! Turn Around! And Follow a New Path!** Then He clearly shows you how to "walk" (Navigate) that path of righteousness.

As courageous as Lt. Hiroo Onoda was, his "perceived" war stole nearly 30 years of his life. Don't let a senseless war that you can never win steal the joy of your salvation! *Fully surrender your heart to Jesus, claim the victory that He won for you and receive HIS righteousness imputed to you by faith! Now that Truth really will Set You Free...Guilt Free!*

What is God's Spirit Saying to Me...
As I Navigate Life According To Galatians

EPHESIANS

Where Most Pastors Won't Go...
When They Start Churches.

Do you know a pastor who's planting a new church? Maybe you'd like to be part of that pioneering work with him. Please, read this and share it with your pastor. ***Without Paul's instructions, it will fail!***

- Where is a good place to plant a new church?
- If you asked the Apostle Paul, where would he send you?
- Six ways to navigate planting a church...from each chapter in Ephesians.

Where Most Pastors Won't Go...
When They Start Churches.

"Okay," the pastor says to his wife, "Where should we begin our new church?" As this idealistic young pastor-and-wife team plans their new ministry, they talk about their options. *"Maybe we should be close to family,"* the wife suggests. *"Sounds good,"* chimes in her husband, *"How about that real nice area of town where it's peaceful, safe and surrounded by strong Christian families and wholesome living." "I agree,"* responds his wife, *"I like that neighborhood. The people are like us and we want our children to grow up with their same race."* On and on they talk, planning out the "perfect" place to plant a church. **But had they lived in the Apostle Paul's day, he would have sent them to one of the wickedest and most convoluted cities on earth...Ephesus!**

Ephesus was a city of extreme mixture. A bastion of races, cultures and religions, it boasted of sensual lifestyles, cult prostitutes and wealth beyond measure. It hosted the great temple of the Greek Goddess, Artemis (Roman name for Diana), daughter of Zeus and the coliseum that seated 25,000 where men fought beasts to the death. And all this debauchery was united under one grand banner...GREED! **But amidst sin's darkness, the light of Christianity sprang up.** Most would have avoided this hostile den of iniquity as a location to plant a church. But not Paul! *To him, Ephesus was fertile ground. There he introduced the inhabitants of this perverse city to a new banner of righteous living and unity...CHRIST!*

So, if you're a pastor planning to start a church...or if you're a parishioner desiring to be part of a pioneering church, **what should you know before you begin your new ministry?** Let's gain insight from each chapter of Paul's letter to the church in Ephesus. Remember that when he wrote this amazing letter...*he was a Prisoner of Rome!*

1. Some People Living In Wicked Places Are <u>PREDESTINED</u> For Righteousness (Eph. 1:3-12). No one fully understands this concept...it's hidden in God's sovereign purposes. But here's your task: find them by preaching Christ's redeeming love and His kind intentions for their lives. *When they respond with repentance, you'll know that God sent you there for them!*

2. There Is <u>NO RACIAL SEGREGATION</u> For Those Who Are In Christ (Eph. 2:11-18; 3:4-10)! If you're afraid your children might date and marry outside their race, don't go to where the Apostle Paul sends you! The Jews became racial supremacists believing that God loved them more than all other races. *The issue has never been about Race...it's about Faith (Gal. 3:28)!*

3. You Can't Plant a Church Without The <u>POWER of Christ's LOVE</u> (Eph. 3:16-21)! The love of God is **Power!** **Power** to love the unlovable. **Power** to be patient when wronged. **Power** to forgive when offended. **Power** to extend mercy and grace when judgment and harshness is deserved. *Power to represent Christ and to reconcile sinners back to God (2 Cor. 5:18-21).*

4. You Can't Do This Without <u>ALL FIVE LEADERSHIP GIFTS</u> At Work (Eph. 4:7-16). It's impossible for all five leadership gifts to reside in just one person. *If you don't expose your congregation to the other four gifts, your church will be deficient in its faith and its maturity.*

5. Make Sure Your <u>OWN</u> <u>FAMILY</u> Is In Proper Order (Eph. 5:21-6:4)! It's not easy building a church. It puts strain on everything...including the pastor's family. Remember, family relationships must reflect the relationship between Christ and His Church. *And the congregation knows if it doesn't!*

6. Don't Forget...You're In a <u>**SPIRITUAL WAR ZONE**</u> (Eph. 6:10-18)! Paul closed out his letter to the Ephesians with the reality of what happens when churches are planted in the midst of evil. *All Hell Breaks Loose!* In other words, you'll quickly discover that a shrewd devil is plotting to discredit and destroy you and the work you're doing! *And the "smart weapon" he uses against you is your own fallen nature!* That's why you need ALL of God's armor to protect you and your ministry!

What is God's Spirit Saying to Me...
As I Navigate Life According To Ephesians

PHILIPPIANS

The Story Behind the Story
What You'll Miss Without It!

We sit in safe, comfortable homes...sipping a good cup of coffee... reading the Bible...and enjoying its truths. *But for Paul and those who worked with him, there wasn't a New Testament! They were writing it through tears and great suffering!*

- What was really going on when Paul wrote his letter to the Philippians?

- What's the "Story Behind The Story" that surrounds some of our familiar passages?

- Once you know the "Story Behind The Story," what should you do with it?

The Story Behind the Story
What You'll Miss Without It!

In our hectic multi-tasking world, it's easy to quickly grab a scripture that sounds good and quote it without realizing the drama that lies behind that passage. But without careful research, the pathos of human suffering that surrounds <u>why</u> a passage was written can be overlooked. In addition, the depth of <u>what</u> it meant to the writer and its recipients can be lost. Here's what I'm talking about:

Confined by Rome as a prisoner of the state, the aging apostle picked up his pen and began to write. Not certain of his fate, Paul wrote, *"Christ will even now, as always, be exalted in my body, whether by life or by death. For to me, to live is Christ and to die is gain"* (Philip. 1:20-21). He who had given his life for the Gospel was ready to die for the faith. ***Yet, in this gentle letter to the Philippian church that he had planted 10 years prior, his desire was to commend and encourage them, not himself.*** Who among us would have been as totally selfless as this great giant of the Christian Faith? ***Now, let's look at the behind-the-scene stories that surround some of our familiar passages.***

1. ***"He who began a good work in you will perfect it until the day of Christ Jesus" (Philip. 1:6).*** Sounds encouraging, doesn't it? But what you may not know is that while Paul was imprisoned, <u>other Christian Preachers were dancing on his grave</u>! (Philip. 1:15-17). Yet in spite of this deplorable reality, Paul rejoiced that, regardless of evil motives, the Gospel was being preached (Philip. 1:12, 18). Paul was convinced that God really does work all things together for good.

2. ***"Work out your salvation with fear and trembling; for it is God who is at work in you, both to will and to work for His good pleasure" (Philip. 2:12-13).*** This describes the anxiety that a person justifiably has when he distrusts his own ability to meet

the requirements of salvation, even though he tries. What you may not know is that **Paul's messenger, Epaphroditus, risked his life and nearly died** in his journey to bring this encouraging letter to the church at Philippi (Philip. 2:25-30). What was the message worth dying for? It was that God helps you to do what pleases Him...because you can't do it by yourself!

3. *"Forgetting what lies behind and reaching forward to what lies ahead, I press on toward the goal for the prize of the upward call of God in Christ Jesus" (Philip. 3:13-14).* Many use this passage as encouragement when starting over from a failure. But that wasn't Paul's point. He tenaciously fought against religious leaders who drew Christians into Jewish Law requiring circumcision for salvation (Philip. 3:2). **Paul "left behind" his confidence that comes by trying to keep the Law. His new confidence was in the True Righteousness that comes only from Christ!** *That was the "Goal" and the "Prize" toward which he was "pressing forward".*

4. *"Be anxious for nothing...I have learned to be content in whatever circumstances I am...I can do all things through Him who strengthens me" (Philip. 4:6, 11, 13).* Oh how casually we use these scriptures to refer to "inconvenient" tasks that we have to endure. But here's the real drama: **Paul wrote this comforting chapter knowing that at any moment he may be beheaded!** Paul's sufferings were beyond our wildest imagination (2 Cor. 11:23-28). Yet the earnest desire of his apostolic heart was to encourage and comfort others. **What a Giant in the Christian Faith!**

So what am I saying? The Bible tells us stories of real human beings who laughed, cried, loved, suffered and died...just like you and me. So take some time out of your busy schedule to discover the *"Story Behind Their Story."* When you do, the passage you read will grip your soul and help you to properly apply its meaning to your own life. Now, read Paul's letter to the Philippians one more time (it's only 4 chapters long). *This time get inside the hearts of those who gave their lives so you can have the Bible. Then the Bible really will become your "MAP" and God's Spirit really will be your "COMPASS!"*

What is God's Spirit Saying to Me...
As I Navigate Life According To Philippians

COLOSSIANS

New-Age Teaching in the Early Church! The Colossian Heresy

Those who will not learn from history are doomed to repeat it. If we, as Christians, do not learn from heresies that invaded the early church, we'll blindly fall into the same error...*unless someone warns us!*

- What was the Colossian Heresy and how is it similar to New Age teaching?
- Five ways to detect heresy if it begins to grow in your church.
- What happens if you buy into theological mixture?

New-Age Teaching in the Early Church!
The Colossian Heresy

"Their talk will spread like gangrene!" That's the way the Apostle Paul described what was happening in the early church (2 Tim. 2:17-18). He was speaking of false teachers who twisted sound doctrine into a perverted gospel. Gangrene is a medical term that describes the death of an area of the body. It develops when the blood supply is cut off through injury or infection which results in cell death. **"Spiritual" Gangrene** is what happens when the life-blood of Biblically sound doctrine is cut off from a believer. It brings spiritual death to those members of the Body of Christ who have been affected. And it was happening in the Colossian church as well. **False doctrine was being sown in the hearts of Christians by mixing Judaism** *(strict laws of Moses),* **Gnosticism** *(higher knowledge based on world philosophies of good and evil)* **and Christianity into a lethal cocktail of religious deception.** Tragically, that heresy wasn't confined to the past...it's relevant, alive and well in churches today!

There are no new deceptions...just new people who buy into ancient lies! The New Age belief system is a free-flowing spiritual movement that adds a smorgasbord of world religions and philosophies to whatever their proponents join themselves to. **Similar to what Bible scholars call "The Colossian Heresy," New Age works by the principle of "mixing" beliefs with Christianity to produce a "Hybrid" faith.** They combine elements of Atheism, Pantheism, Buddhism, Taoism, Hinduism, Islam, Gnosticism, Spiritualism, and Universalism with the precious truths of Christianity. The end result is the "Different Gospel" that Paul warned the early church about (2 Cor. 11:4; Gal. 1:6). *The Colossian Heresy and New Age are deceptive cousins...they invade Christianity like slow spreading Gangrene!*

So, my friends, how can you recognize Heresy if it begins to grow in your church? Consider this:

1. **It Tampers With the Person of Jesus.** No place in scripture will you find a more profound and precise statement of the doctrine of the Person of Christ than in Colossians (Col. 1:15-20; 2:9-10). *Any teaching that detracts from His deity as the <u>ONE</u> and <u>ONLY</u> Christ is total heresy!*

2. **It Mixes World Religions with Christianity Claiming That All Religions Are Acceptable to God.** At the heart of the Colossian Heresy was theological mixture. If anyone tells you God accepts everybody regardless of what they believe, that's gangrene! *If you don't personally <u>BELIEVE</u> in Jesus as the Son of God who died and rose again for your salvation, you're lost (John 3:18-21: Mark 16:16)!*

3. **It Claims "Higher" Knowledge that Allows People to Live Extreme Lifestyles.** Paul denounced Gnostic beliefs that offered two extremes...extreme self-abasement (Col. 2:20-23) or extreme moral liberation (Col. 3:5-8). *Neither is taught in Scripture. Run from these, my friend!*

4. **It Emphasizes Philosophical Wisdom Over Redemptive Wisdom.** All religions have moral and philosophical truth. But only in God's Son can you find Redemption (Col. 1:9-14; 2:8-15). *Any teaching that moves your faith away from the Gospel is deceptive and ends in death (Col. 1:23)!*

5. **It Subtly Moves You Into Idolatry.** Most Christians would agree with Paul's rejection of the worship of angels (Col. 2:18-19). *Yet those who buy into New Age will personify "The Universe" and speak as if <u>IT</u> controlled people's lives instead of God! That, my friend, is IDOLATRY!*

How then can you navigate your life according to the "Map" of Colossians? Stay clear of any teaching that weaves world religions into the Christian faith. *It ultimately leads to destruction and removal from the Tree of Life (Rev. 22:18-19)!* And how can you navigate your life by the "Compass" of God's Spirit? He will ALWAYS point you to faith in Jesus as your ONLY way of salvation (John 16:13-15). *If you continue in rebellion and ignore His direction, you'll grieve the Holy Spirit (Eph. 4:30)! Then, tragically, God will allow you to believe a lie because you would not receive the truth (2 Thess. 2:10-12)!*

What is God's Spirit Saying to Me...
As I Navigate Life According To Colossians

1 THESSALONIANS

"Christ-Mass" Is What Happens...
When Christmas Is Over

"What a Big Fat Let-Down!" That's what many people (even some Christians) say when the Christmas season is over. *But what if I told you that December 26th is just the <u>Beginning</u> of your ministry!*

- What does the book of 1 Thessalonians have to do with the Christmas season?
- Where did the name, "Christmas," come from?
- Five ways to Begin your ministry AFTER Christmas is over.

"Christ-Mass" Is What Happens...
When Christmas Is Over

Actually, the classic Christmas season that we enjoy each year didn't exist during the first 300 years of Christianity. However, there are key ingredients in Paul's first letter to the church in Thessalonica that bring our merriment back into proper focus...especially when it's over.

The weeks leading up to Christmas are filled with festive decorations, excitement, family gatherings and surprise gifts for our loved ones. And what prompts this joyous occasion? *"For unto you is born a Savior who is Christ the Lord!"* It's the celebration of God who became flesh and grew up to become our Savior. He showed us who God really is and how much He really loves us. We celebrate because without the Savior's Birth, Death and Resurrection, we would be forever lost in sin and estranged from God. *But unfortunately, after the celebration is over, the presents unwrapped and the Christmas trees discarded...we return to the same old humdrum way of life.* So what's the point? If we're not <u>DIFFERENT</u> after Christmas...then maybe we've missed what "Christ-Mass" is supposed to be.

The term "Christmas" is not found in the Bible. It comes from a compound English word for "Christ's Mass"...which is the celebration of the Eucharist in liturgical churches. But the term "mass" is derived from the Latin word "missa" which simply means *"Dismissal"*. *As Christianity grew, "Mass" took on a deeper meaning...it's the missionary nature of God's Church in the world.* <u>*It's you and me living out our faith for the world to see!*</u>

Paul wrote his first letter to the believers in Thessalonica to encourage this fledgling church in their walk with the Lord. Under great persecution from the Jews and fleshly influences from pagans, they were slipping back to their old ways of life...just as if they had never known Jesus! They needed this inspired letter to guide them <u>AFTER</u>

the Savior had come into their lives. And so do we! *"Christ-Mass" is Jesus sending (dismissing) us into the world AFTER we celebrate His birth on Christmas Day. What then should we do on December 26th? Consider this:*

1. After Christmas...Walk With Spiritual Integrity (1 Thess. 2:11-12). We, who are called to live both in God's Kingdom and in the world, must live our faith for the world to see. Our faith is in God who sent His Son to redeem us back to Himself. *When the world sees our honest humility before the Lord and our repentant hearts, we become witnesses of His gracious redeeming love.*

2. After Christmas...Pursue Your Destiny No Matter What (1 Thess. 2:17-18). Paul's experience in Thessalonica was more than most of us could handle. He was violently run out of town (Acts 17:1-10)! Yet, he refused to be discouraged...even when thwarted by Satan himself (1 Thess. 2:18)! *Tenaciously pursue your calling, my Christian friend! And if it's temporarily delayed...don't give up!*

3. After Christmas...Live a Life That's Pleasing to the Lord (1 Thess. 4:1-8). Like the Thessalonians, it's easy to slip back into old ways of living. *Read this passage carefully and re-commit yourself to righteous living. No one is sinless...but we must resist sin at all costs!*

4. After Christmas...Live With Confidence Knowing That Christ Will Return Soon (1 Thess. 1:9-10; 4:13-18; 5:2-9). Unfortunately, some use these scriptures to try to "scare" people into repentance before Jesus returns. Paul wrote these passages to **ENCOURAGE** believers, not make them fearful! *If Jesus is your Savior, He's coming back to Glorify you...not punish you!*

5. **After Christmas...Keep the Fire of the Holy Spirit Burning (1 Thess. 5:19-22).** The Holy Spirit is The GIFT that Jesus sent into the hearts of His believers (John 14:16-17; Acts 2:38-39). He gently guides you, corrects you and speaks into your life through prophetic utterances. *Whatever you do, DON'T insult the Spirit of Grace (Heb. 10:29)! Without His "Fire" burning in your life, you're on your own without God in a very cold and dark world!*

So, my friends, what happens after December 25th? *Your ministry in the world just begins!*

What is God's Spirit Saying to Me...
As I Navigate Life According To 1 Thessalonians

2 THESSALONIANS

Okay, So the Mayan Calendar Was Wrong When Will the World <u>Really</u> End?

We survived "Y2K"...but what happened to "Doomsday 2012?" The superstitious look to predictions from ancient cultures; the faithful look to God; and the cynical think its foolishness! ***But what did Paul think about the End of the World?***

- What was this "2012 Mayan Calendar" flap all about?
- Why were the Thessalonians concerned about the End of the World?
- How can Paul's letters to the early church help us understand when the world will end?

Okay, So the Mayan Calendar Was Wrong When Will the World <u>Really</u> End?

Cosmic Re-alignment! Killer Asteroids! Catastrophic Earthquakes! World Decimating Tsunamis! That's also how the over-the-top *2012* movie said it might happen. The old world would be swept away and a New World would be born. So, what was the basis of that "ultimate disaster" Hollywood storyline that was released in 2009? It was the Mayan Calendar. And who were the Mayans? They were pagans who worshipped everything in nature and tried to predict the future according to a complex set of astrological calendars. *The Mayan gods were forces of nature and animal spirits that could be made happy by sacrifice...even human sacrifices! Well, so much for the credibility of Mayan predictions!*

The church in Thessalonica didn't know anything about a Mayan Calendar that predicted a 2012 Doomsday. But they <u>were</u> worried about a different kind of calamity...**<u>Suffering</u>** and **<u>Death</u>**! Though they looked forward to Christ ushering in a New World when He returns, they still had questions. In the midst of extreme persecution mixed with false teaching, many were fearful and confused. The Apostle Paul quieted their fears and brought clarity to their misunderstanding with two letters he wrote to them. *Here were their questions and Paul's answers: Perhaps you've wondered about these as well?*

1. **What's the Mystery of Death and Life After Death?** Well-meaning Christians in Thessalonica had a great concern. They were afraid that the believers who had died <u>before</u> the Lord's return would be left out of that glorious event. Paul reassured them that Jesus, who died and rose again, would bring with Him all Christians who had previously died (1 Thess. 4:13-18). *Sorry, Mayans. Your New World pales in comparison to our Reality in Christ!*

2. **Is Suffering a Sign of a Lack of Spirituality?** In other words, what does a righteous God think about suffering and will He do anything about it? The church in Thessalonica was birthed in persecution and the people wondered if it would ever stop (Acts 17:1-8). Paul's revelation was totally beyond Mayan theology. *God allowed suffering because He considered their perseverance and faith to be worthy of His Kingdom. God was working with them and would certainly bring justice. He said He would "repay with affliction those who afflict you" (2 Thess. 1:4-12).*

3. **When Will The World Come to an End?** False teachers were leading believers astray saying the "Day of the Lord" (the End Times) had already come. Paul corrected that heresy by revealing that it has NOTHING to do with persecution or catastrophic events of nature. *It happens with <u>Apostasy</u>...the falling away of believers from the faith (1 Thess. 2:1-12; Matt. 24:3-14)! You don't have to look to a Mayan Calendar for that one. It's already happening in God's Church...even today!*

4. **How Should We Be Living Knowing That the World Will One Day Come to an End?** In the *2012* movie, people built a colossal boat to survive the catastrophic floods that would destroy the earth. (Hmm...sounds a bit like Gen. 6-9.) But Paul's instructions were much more comforting. *Don't be afraid...you are <u>Not</u> destined for wrath (1 Thess. 5:1-11). Stand firm knowing God has chosen you for salvation and glory at His coming (2 Thess. 2:13-15). Love God, live a responsible life and walk in His peace (2 Thess. 3:5-16).*

So, what about the Mayan prediction? They were absolutely WRONG about a 2012 Doomsday! If you're in Christ, you can live each year with Purpose and Destiny in Him! **And you don't have to wait until Christ returns to have a New Beginning.** *It happened the day you believed in Jesus and trusted your life into His hands!*

What is God's Spirit Saying to Me...
As I Navigate Life According To 2 Thessalonians

1 TIMOTHY

You Say You Believe in God... But Does God Believe in You?

Most people focus on their faith in God, which they should. But very few would even consider asking the question, "Does God believe in me?" *Unless He does, it's impossible to represent Christ in the world.*

- What does "believe" really mean?
- Why is it important for God to believe in you?
- Four ways to know if God believes in you or not.

You Say You Believe in God...
But Does God Believe in You?

"Does God believe in me?" That's the question Susan Sarandon's character asked in the 2008 movie, "Autumn Hearts." It's a story of a woman who lives in the past and can't escape the trauma of a Nazi internment camp during WWII. Her question is certainly intriguing, but it's a thinly veiled intent to criticize God. **What she's saying is, "Faith doesn't work for me...it's a one-way street for God's benefit only."** In other words, *"Now look here, God. I've put out a lot of effort into believing that You're real, so why do You let bad things happen to me?"* What this lady didn't know is that God WANTS to "Believe" in people...but it's neither automatic nor universal. The Lord has certain criteria He looks for BEFORE He can "Believe" in you.

So what does "Believe" mean? The same Greek word that is translated as "Believe" can also be translated as *"Have Faith In; Have Confidence In; Trust; and Be Fully Trustworthy."* Belief isn't a casual acknowledgement or just a general thought process. **It's a powerful conviction!** Jesus may be the "Potential" Savior of the world, but He is the "Effectual" Savior only for those who personally and totally believe and place their trust in the redemptive work of the Son of God (John 3:18; Mark 16:16).

Christianity is NOT a Religion; it's a Relationship with the Living God...which requires mutual commitment, trust and affection. Before God can "believe" (place His confidence in and His trust) in people, they must show themselves to be TRUSTWORTHY of God's gift of salvation. As you read Paul's first letter to his young protégé, Timothy, it becomes more than obvious that God believed in both Paul and Timothy. So what does it take for God to believe in you? Consider this:

1. He Does <u>Not</u> Trust Those Who Have Not Fixed Their Hope On The Living God (1 Tim. 4:10 NASB). Sure, God is sovereign and can do all things...with or without people's involvement. But He desires to "partner" with people to represent His cause in the earth (John 17:14-26). *Those who refuse to trust in His Son's sacrifice have no relationship with God at all (Matt. 7:23)!*

2. God Trusts Those Who Tenaciously Guard The Truth of The Gospel (1 Tim. 1:11-17). As the commentator, K. S. Wuest, wrote, *"God saw that the fiery, zealous, intense Pharisee would be just as fiery, zealous, and intense in the proclamation of the gospel as he was in its persecution, when saving grace was operating in his being. God demonstrated His confidence in Paul by putting him into the ministry."* Paul would not tolerate false doctrines to be taught in God's Church. *That's why Paul pressed Timothy to Guard the Faith at all costs (1 Tim. 6:20-21)!*

3. God Trusts Hearts That Pray For Their Enemies (1 Tim. 2:1-8). In the midst of Nero's insane cruelty and slaughter of Christian believers, Paul instructed Timothy to *"pray for all who are in authority,"* which included Nero himself! *God trusts those who think like He does...desiring to restore even the vilest of sinners (Matt. 5:43-45; Luke 6:35-36).*

4. God Trusts Church Leaders Who Are Filled With Integrity...in Their Personal Lives (1 Tim. 3:1-13; 4:12-16). Paul placed an enormous trust in Timothy to organize the church in Ephesus. What criteria was Timothy to look for in setting forth church leaders? Right living and proper management of their households. *Integrity is not a sinless life...it's a forgiven life in complete relationship with God.*

And now, back to the question, "Does God Believe in you?" ***Absolutely YES...<u>IF</u> you show yourself trustworthy over your precious salvation that God graciously gives to you.*** That, my friend, is how you navigate your Destiny according to the "Map" of Paul's first letter to Timothy. Now the "Compass" of God's Spirit can lead you to represent Christ in the world...right where you live.

What is God's Spirit Saying to Me...
As I Navigate Life According To 1 Timothy

2 TIMOTHY

Leaving a Legacy of Destiny... For Your Great-Great-Grandchildren!

What will your family look like 100 years from now? Few people ever think that far in the future...much less plan for it. But now YOU can! ***Whether you realize it or not, YOU will determine their Destiny!***

- What is a Legacy?
- How many people can a Legacy affect?
- Four ways to build a Legacy that will influence your Great-Great-Grandchildren...yet to be born.

Leaving a Legacy of Destiny...
For Your Great-Great-Grandchildren!

When I spoke the final words over my Dad...I reflected on what he had taught me about life and how to be a good husband and a father. Seven years later, I did the same for my mother. She loved me more than life itself and taught me about excellence. Residing within me are their character traits and my childhood memories that have guided me throughout life. And now that legacy is being passed on to our children and grandchildren. And so it goes...each generation passes on to the next the substance of their lives...both good and not-so-good. We can learn from both; discarding the useless and embracing the precious for the next generation to follow. *Legacy...It's your life extended into the lives of your children and all their generations that follow. It's a path through life's jungles for others to follow.*

When the final curtain fell over the Apostle Paul's life, what did he leave his children? As far as we know, he had no biological sons or daughters. Yet during his life, he had many spiritual sons. And now, nearly 2000 years later, <u>billions</u> have embraced his fathering spirit. Paul's second letter to Timothy was his last recorded writing while he was alive. Sensing this was his farewell address, he wrote, *"The time of my departure has come. I have fought the good fight; I have finished the course; I have kept the faith."* Through tears, Timothy read the last letter he would ever receive from Paul, his spiritual dad. *By walking side-by-side with Paul, he received a pattern for passing on the legacy he received from this great man of God. And so can you!*

1. Teach Your Children About <u>SPIRITUAL GENETICS</u> (2 Tim. 1:5-6). Faith is the capacity to believe God in the midst of contradictory and adversarial circumstances. Though salvation can't be inherited from parents, God's favor can! Listen to His promise... *"Therefore know that the Lord your God, He is God, the faithful God who keeps covenant and mercy for a*

Thousand Generations *with those who love Him and keep His commandments" (Deut. 7:9).*

2. Teach the Next Generation to <u>GUARD</u> the Treasures of God (2 Tim. 1:13-14). Some inheritances are houses, lands and money. When a godly man or woman leaves an inheritance, it most certainly should include possessions, but also something infinitely more precious...**God's Treasures of Redemptive Truth and Eternal Life!** Unless this treasure is guarded at all costs, it can be stolen away. *Read Matt. 13:19-23 to discover how this can happen to you!*

3. Train Them To Properly <u>READ</u> and <u>UNDERSTAND</u> the <u>BIBLE</u> (2 Tim. 2:15; 3:15-17). Medical malpractice can cause injury or physical death. Biblical Malpractice can cause spiritual injury and eternal death! *In Paul's day, false teachers distorted scripture for personal gain and led people into deception (2 Tim. 3:2-7; 4:3-4). Don't think that can't happen to you and to them!*

4. Show Them How To Handle Life's <u>SUCCESSES</u> and <u>FAILURES</u>. In Paul's first letter, he told Timothy how a financially successful person should handle their wealth (1 Tim. 6:9-10, 17-19). In his second letter, he helped Timothy know how to deal with his emotional weaknesses and how to suffer hardships (2 Tim. 1:6-9; 2:3-5). And should he fail morally, Paul told him how to cleanse himself (2 Tim. 2:20-26). *Oh, how you and I need Paul's fathering spirit today!*

"But," you may respond, *"My parents never left me a legacy like that. So what do I have to give my children?"* When you received Christ as your Savior, He gave you an infinitely better inheritance...**His Spirit!** *With the Holy Spirit as the "Compass" of your life and the Bible as your "Map," you can build a spiritual legacy for all to see.* By following Paul's example, you will be instrumental in forming the Destinies of your Great-Great-Grandchildren yet to be born!

What is God's Spirit Saying to Me...
As I Navigate Life According To 2 Timothy

TITUS

Starting a Church the WRONG Way! The Flip Side of Titus

Across 35 years of pastoral ministry, I've seen glorious successes and colossal failures. *A church collapse is usually attributed to one major problem...failure to stick with the Fundamentals of Christianity.*

- What does football have to do with churches?
- What does the book of Titus have to do with starting a church?
- Four ways to begin a church that will most certainly end in TOTAL FAILURE!

Starting a Church the WRONG Way!
The Flip Side of Titus

Football in hand, Vince Lombardi walked to the front of the room, took several seconds to look over the people in silence, held out the pigskin in front of him, and said, *"Gentlemen, this is a football."* In only five words, Lombardi communicated his point: **We're going to start with the basics and make sure we're executing all the fundamentals.** With that, the Green Bay Packers began to dominate the NFL during the decade of the 1960s. But what if the Packers had not followed Lombardi's leadership and had done the exact opposite? They would have remained in last place as the laughing stock of the NFL! *If this is true for football, how much more are Fundamentals needed when a pastor begins a Christian Church?*

Starting a church in America today is a "piece of cake" compared to Paul's day. Steeped in Judaism, pagan lifestyles and violence, the nations rejected, persecuted and killed those who spread Christianity in the Middle East. So, when Paul sent Titus to the island of Crete to oversee the fledgling Christian churches, he wanted to make certain it was done right. In three short chapters of this letter he wrote to Titus, he outlined the **Basics** and the **Fundamentals** on how to begin a church the **RIGHT** way. *But if a pastor doesn't read Titus or chooses to ignore its truths, the church he/she plants will fail miserably and embarrass the cause of God.* That's why I'm giving you the "Flip Side" of Titus. Here's what **NOT** to do:

1. Begin **WITHOUT** Mature Counsel and Oversight. *In other words...Don't have a "Paul" in your life (Titus 1:1-4)!* Paul didn't just call himself an apostle of Jesus Christ...he was one! Young pastors have zeal and vision, but they lack wisdom that only comes through experience and proven ministry. *Unless you have seasoned eldership actively overseeing your ministry and giving you counsel, both you and those who follow you will*

most certainly fall into a pit...a pit that you didn't even know was there (Luke 6:39)!

2. Begin <u>BEFORE</u> You Develop the Godly Character of a True Elder. In reality, pastors are the elders of their churches. But you can't oversee the work of your church by yourself. You need spiritual men and women, seasoned in God's word, to work with you as a council of elders. So what's the character of a true elder? *Carefully read Titus 1:5-9 to discover the criteria that Paul gave Titus. Then judge yourself. (Warning...it takes <u>Years</u> to develop this kind of character!)*

3. Be So <u>OPEN-MINDED</u> That You Fail To Guard the Faith. Paul was a "barracuda" when it came to dealing with false teachers who spread heresy among the flock. He called them "Savage Wolves" (Acts 20:28-31)! There's a demonic trend in today's churches to accept all religions as equally true. They believe "The Christ" lives in ALL people, regardless of what they believe. *I implore you, read the following passages to see how false that statement really is: Matt. 24:4-5, 23-25; Eph. 4:11-16; 2 Tim. 2:16-18; 3:1-9; Titus 1:10-16; Jude 4-16.*

4. <u>FORGET</u> That You're a Christian and Just Live Any Way You Want! In Paul's letter to Titus, he delivered the <u>Basics</u> and the <u>Fundamentals</u> of the Christian Faith. These very clearly spell out how a Christian should live. First of all, Christianity is NOT a Religion...it's a personal relationship with Jesus, the Savior (Titus 2:13; 3:3-7; 1 Cor. 1:9)! Secondly, even though salvation is not based on works, God really does have standards for how Christians should live and treat one another (Titus 2:1-15; 3:9-11). *Throw away these and your church will self-destruct and collapse from its own weight!*

So, if you want your church to FAIL, just do the opposite of what Paul taught. *But if you navigate your life and ministry according to the principles found in Titus, you've started␣out the right way. It's as simple as that!*

What is God's Spirit Saying to Me...
As I Navigate Life According To Titus

PHILEMON

When Christians HATE One Another!
A Strategy for Reconciliation

Do you have friends who are angry enough to HATE one another? Would you like to bring reconciliation to their relationship? ***Don't try it until you read this teaching!***

- Conflict is part of life...but what happens when two people who are CHRISTIANS hate one another?

- The deadly progression of an offense. Stop it before it goes too far!

- Six ingredients of a successful intervention and reconciliation.

When Christians HATE One Another!
A Strategy for Reconciliation

Christians have fallen natures...just like everyone else in the world. When **OFFENSES** escalate beyond levels of tolerance, it can result in **FRUSTRATION, CONFLICT** and **HURT**. If these are not properly resolved, it can produce **ANGER**. If anger isn't dealt with God's way, it creates **VENGEANCE**. If the desire to "get even" isn't stopped dead in its tracks, it gives way to **DEPRESSION, ILLNESS** and/or **VIOLENCE!** Knowing that two of Paul's dearest friends were headed down this deadly path, he penned an amazing letter that gives us a Strategy for Reconciling two warring believers.

Philemon was a well-to-do Christian hosting a church in his home in Colossae. Having been converted to Christianity by Paul, he and his family were personal friends with the aged apostle. As with many wealthy men in those days, Philemon owned slaves. As repugnant as slavery is to the modern world, it was a way of life inextricably woven into the socio-economic world of the first century. Though God never approves of humans owning other humans, the fact remained that some slavery was voluntary. Indigents and people in debt could willingly sell themselves into slavery to escape their predicament. Whatever the case, Onesimus was one of his slaves. ***Then the drama begins: Onesimus stole from his master and ran away. But the plot thickens when the runaway slave met Paul in prison and became a Christian. Now what?!***

Here's what might have been going on in **Onesimus'** mind, *"I'm fed up with this life! I'll take what I need, run away, start a new life and I'm never going back there again!"* **Philemon** might have thought, *"You belonged to me by law! You took what is mine and ran away! I'll hunt you down, punish you and make you pay!"* ***What should Onesimus do now that he's a Christian? And how should Philemon act as a***

Christian toward a new "brother" in the Lord? Interesting Dilemma, isn't it?!

1. Intervention Begins When Both Parties <u>TRUST</u> the Reconciler. Trust means you are confident that you will be treated in fairness and honesty with no hidden biases. If one feels that they'll get a "raw deal," everything falls apart. *Both Onesimus and Philemon trusted Paul with their very lives.*

2. There Has to Have Been Emotional and Spiritual <u>DEPOSITS</u> Made Into Warring Factions. Both Onesimus and Philemon owed their eternal salvation to Paul's love for them and his ministry of the Gospel (Philem. 10, 19). *That kind of leverage isn't self-serving...it's redemptive!*

3. If You're Looking for a Godly Strategy for Intervention and Reconciliation, Read Carefully What Paul Did!

    - <u>COMPLIMENT</u> Instead of Condemn *(Philem. 4-7)*. If you begin an intervention by chiding, it shuts down receptivity and closes hearts to reconciliation. Paul began his letter by truthfully giving appreciation for Philemon's character and ministry. *That's called wisdom!*

    - <u>APPEAL</u> Rather Than Dictate *(Philem. 8-14)*. Paul could have rightfully used his apostolic authority to demand (and command) Philemon to accept his runaway slave as his brother in Christ. *But instead, Paul appealed to Philemon on the basis of his love for them both.*

    - <u>INFUSE</u> God's Love Into Hardened Hearts *(Philem. 15-21)*. God's love is more than a feel good emotion. *It Transforms Lives!* It makes a runaway slave embrace the master he once hated. It makes a slave owner repent and change his values. *And it can do the same for you!*

Does this strategy always work? No...not if there are strong-willed and unprincipled people involved. *But is it worth it to try? Absolutely YES! Reconciliation is in the very heart of God. And you, my friend, are called to the ministry of Reconciliation (2 Cor. 5:17-21)!*

What is God's Spirit Saying to Me...
As I Navigate Life According To Philemon

HEBREWS

A New and Improved Christianity That's Called MIXTURE!

It's amazing how history repeats itself. There's a deadly trend in many churches today that the early church also struggled with. ***They want to be so Relevant and Inclusive that they've lost their Saltiness!***

- What is Theological Mixture?
- What does the book of Hebrews have to do with Mixture?
- Four Absolutes of the Christian Faith...without which, you would no longer be a Christian!

A New and Improved Christianity That's Called MIXTURE!

Would you drink water that's 95% pure? That's the question my civil engineering professor asked as I began a course in Waste Treatment in 1967. The students just sat there in silence knowing that whatever answer we gave would probably be wrong. Finally he answered his own question by saying, *"If you did, you may be dead in 24 hours!"* That's when I first learned that MIXTURE CAN KILL YOU!

Forty years later, I've seen with my own eyes that <u>THEOLOGICAL MIXTURE</u> is even more deadly than sewer water. *It can contaminate your spirit and disqualify you from eternal salvation!* That's what happens when a Christian church decides to "mix" world religions into the doctrines of the Christian Faith and call it a New and Improved Christianity! *And that's what was happening in the early church nearly 2,000 years ago.*

Soon after the Christian church was birthed, Jewish Christians began mixing the Old Covenant that God made with Moses (including the sacrificial system) into the New Covenant in Christ...while professing Jesus as their Savior. That was precisely why a letter was written, warning them of the dangers of theological mixture. That letter is now a book in the Bible we call "Hebrews." The writer (most believe it was Paul) confronted their misconceptions by separating truth from <u>mixture</u>. He did this by systematically laying the theological foundations of the Christian Faith. *Without these absolute truths, we would no longer be Christians and our faith would be worthless!*

1. **Jesus Is Preeminent Over All Religious Leaders of the World (Heb. 1-4).** Jewish Christians in the early church were <u>mixing</u> Moses and the Laws with Christianity. But Jesus is infinitely greater than Moses and even the angels themselves. He's not a philosophical leader that decided to start a religion...He's God!

Regardless of how you try to say that all religions lead to God, you can't "Improve" on the fact that Jesus IS GOD who became flesh! *You cannot get to God without Jesus (John 14:6-11)...end of story!*

2. **Jesus Does NOT Make Salvation "Automatic" (Heb. 3-4).** The Jews thought that because they were children of Abraham, God automatically accepted them. They were mistaken (Matt. 3:9-10)! Don't be deceived by thinking that Jesus' death and resurrection has saved the whole world regardless of what they believe. *Without an active and personal faith in Jesus as the Son of God who died and rose for you, you do not have eternal salvation (John 3:16-21; Mark 16:16)!*

3. **Nothing Connects You To God Like Jesus' Covenant (Heb. 8)!** God created people to love, to share Himself with and to fulfill His purposes on earth. The relationship between God and humankind is facilitated through an agreement called Covenant. The Jewish Christians were mixing the Old Covenant sacrifices with the redemptive work of God's Son. *Jesus' Covenant is infinitely superior because He fulfilled ALL the conditions of redemption for us. He was our sacrifice! All we have to do is believe in what He did for us. No...You can't improve on that!*

4. **But Salvation Doesn't Mean You Can Live Any Way You Want (Heb. 12-13)!** Pagan influences from the nations were being mixed into the lifestyles of Christians. No, you can't be redeemed from the penalty of sin by behavior modification. But neither can you belligerently ignore God's standards for living. *The writer of Hebrews gave the solution: Fix your eyes on Jesus, live responsibly and grow into maturity as a redeemed man or woman of God!*

So, my friends, the Book of Hebrews is an essential "Navigational" document for your life. It points you to Jesus...the Author and

Finisher of your faith. *For without it, you can drift off course...and some may even miss heaven (Heb. 6:4-8)!*

What is God's Spirit Saying to Me...
As I Navigate Life According To Hebrews

JAMES

YOU Call Yourself a CHRISTIAN? HA!
Straight Talk by Jesus' Brother!

Christians live in glass houses...and the world sees us and expects us to be "Perfect." So what are the standards that God requires of us? *James doesn't hold back. He tells it like it is!*

- What was going on that caused James to write his letter to the churches?
- How is a REAL Christian supposed to act?
- So...what happens when you fall short of God's standards?

YOU Call Yourself a CHRISTIAN? HA! Straight Talk by Jesus' Brother!

"And YOU call yourself a CHRISTIAN? HA!" Ever had that accusation thrown in your face? If you have, it can cut you to your heart, put you on a mega guilt-trip and stir up anger all at the same time. Some people say it just to hurt you because you wouldn't do what they want you to do. Others sarcastically say it when they vehemently disagree with your stand on moral, social or political issues. However, if that remark really does hit home, it can cause you to re-evaluate your actions and make changes to your character. *But when Christians in the early church read this "straight talk" letter from James, it brought conviction and repentance rather than insult and injury.* And if YOU read it with an open heart, it can be a reality check to judge your own Christian walk as well.

Who was this "James" who penned this remarkable letter? Most Bible scholars agree he was the oldest half-brother of our Lord Jesus. James was also the leader of the Judean church...a no-nonsense kind of a guy. He saw straight through hypocrisy and pretense. Like a skilled surgeon, he diagnosed cancerous issues in the human soul and removed them with carefully directed words from the Lord. I'm sure you've heard this said before: *"God's Church isn't a Country Club for Saints...it's a Hospital for Sinners."* James wrote his straight-talk letter because Christians were spiritually and morally sick. *He wasn't being sarcastic...he was addressing the Christian community whose behavior was consistently beneath God's standards for their lives.* (By the way, I encourage you to read the Introduction to James in the Message Bible. It's a real eye opener!) So...how should you navigate your life according to the book of James?

1. Be the "Master" of Your Trials and Temptations...Not the "Victim" (James 1:2-18)! Persecution, affliction and suffering surrounded the early church. James considered them as

"Trials" that prove faith and loyalty to God. And so it can be with you. ***No, God doesn't cause suffering in your life. But if you endure it with faith, God rewards you with the Crown of Life!***

2. Put Your Actions Where Your Mouth Is (James 1:22-27)! Being a Christian IS Easy...<u>IF</u> you aren't selfish, headstrong, controlling and greedy! It's especially easy if you don't enjoy sin! So, James gives all of us a reality check. ***If you're going to call yourself a Christian, you'd better act like one.*** That means you must discipline yourself for righteous living. Here's how you do it:

- Control Your Emotions...*They can get you into big trouble!* (James 1:19-21)

- Don't Play Favorites Based on Outward Appearances...*God looks at hearts!* (James 2:1-13)

- Make Your Faith ALIVE...*With works that represent what you believe!* (James 2:14-26)

- Guard Your Tongue...*If you don't, you'll destroy people!* (James 3:1-12)

- Demonstrate God's Wisdom...*It's pure, peaceful, gentle and merciful without hypocrisy!* (James 3:13-18)

- Stop Fighting and Hurting Each Other...*You're acting like the world!* (James 4:1-17)

- Be Careful About Wealth...*It can poison your character!* (James 5:1-6)

- Practice Being Patient with People...*Remember, the Lord is patient with you!* (James 5:7-12)

- Pray For the Sick...*God wants to heal people through your prayers! (James 5:13-18)*

- Restore People who Stray from the Truth...*That's what God did for you! (James 5:19-20)*

So, <u>YOU</u> Call Yourself A <u>CHRISTIAN</u>? Absolutely Yes! That's why you should navigate your life according to James. **But what happens when you FAIL to live up to these standards?** That, my friend, is exactly why you <u>NEED</u> to be a Christian. Godly sorrow coupled with repentance (changing) puts you back on track with God (2 Cor. 7:9-10). *Yes, Jesus met the requirements for salvation for those who believe. However, we must line up our lives with His will.* <u>*But if you refuse...maybe you're NOT a Christian at all?*</u>

What is God's Spirit Saying to Me...
As I Navigate Life According To James

___

___

___

___

___

___

___

1 PETER

Peter, Is That Really You? How God's Grace Can Transform <u>ANYBODY</u>!

Have you ever known someone whose life was dramatically transformed by God? Ever wondered what happened? It's all about GRACE! *Don't miss this teaching!*

- What was Peter like BEFORE He received God's Grace?
- What does God's Grace do for you?
- Can you receive more of God's Grace in your life?

Peter, Is That Really You?
How God's Grace Can Transform <u>ANYBODY</u>!

Umm...aren't you the same guy who DENIED ever knowing Jesus? And come to think of it, you denied Him <u>THREE</u> times! I also heard that Jesus had to <u>REBUKE</u> you to your face and said, *"Get behind Me Satan!"* (Matt. 16:21-23). Yeah...and you were so <u>JUDGMENTAL</u> that you tried to <u>THROW JOHN UNDER THE BUS</u> and Jesus had to rebuke you again (John 21:19-23)! <u>BUT</u>...then you stood up and preached with power on the Day of Pentecost (Acts 2:14-40)! <u>Then</u>, God used you to heal a paralyzed man and even to raise a dead person back to life again (Acts 9:32-42)! And <u>Now</u> you're writing this powerful letter to Christians who are suffering? **So, what happened to you?!**

Grace is not Mercy...it's <u>Power</u>! It's God's <u>Power</u> that brings salvation (Eph. 2:8). It's God's <u>Power</u> that gifts us to serve Him (Rom. 12:6-8). It's God's <u>Power</u> that strengthens us to endure suffering (2 Cor. 12:7-10). The grace of God that transforms lives is beyond our ability to figure out! It seems that God delights in turning failures into successes. He takes the "throw-aways" of society and makes them "keepers" for His glory. When the grace of God comes into our lives, everything changes! *When you read Peter's letter, you can see the difference in his life. The Holy Spirit transformed this outspoken, brassy, cursing fisherman into a fearless leader of the Christian Church. Look what He can do for you!*

1. **God's Grace Transforms Fear Into Courage.** You wouldn't want to have been a Christian in 64AD. Believers were burned alive and thrown to beasts for sport. But the same Peter who was once fearful of suffering with Jesus (Matt. 26:57-75) was ready to suffer and even <u>DIE</u> for his faith in Jesus. Faith is the channel through which God's grace flows. *Trust God, my*

friend, and His grace will strengthen you for whatever trial you're facing (Ps. 56:3-4; 1 Pet. 1:3-12)!

2. **God's Grace Transforms Human Friendships Into God's Unconditional Love.** In John 21:15-17 Jesus asked Peter three times if he "loved" Him. The word Jesus used was "agape," which is the unconditional love of God. All three times Peter could only respond with the Greek word "Philos," which is merely human friendship. After the Holy Spirit transformed Peter, he used "agape" over and over when referring to loving God and one another (1 Pet. 1:8; 4:8). *Want to love like Jesus loves? Let God's Spirit transform you by His grace...and you will (Rom. 12:2)!*

3. **God's Grace Transforms Retaliation Into a Quiet Testimony of Faith.** With sword in hand, Peter tried to slice open a man who came to arrest Jesus (John 18:10-11). But after God's grace filled his heart, he spoke of <u>REJOICING</u> in the face of suffering instead of retaliating (1 Pet. 4:12-14). Has someone offended you? Are you being unfairly treated at work? *If you retaliate, you may have some personal satisfaction. But if you suffer for what is right, it refines your faith (1 Pet. 1:7) and gains favor with God (1 Pet. 2:18-23). Grace makes all the difference!*

So, my friend, if God transformed Peter's life, He can transform yours as well. But here's the question that must be asked, *"How Can I Receive More of God's Grace in My Life?"* Consider this:

1. **You Can't "Earn" Grace.** If you're a Christian, God has already freely extended His grace to you (Eph. 1:2-9)!

2. **God Gives You <u>ALL</u> the Grace You Need.** But it's in proportion to the dimension and requirements of your calling and assignment in Him (Acts 4:33; 2 Cor. 9:8; 1 Tim. 1:13-15).

3. **But Be Careful!** God holds you responsible to wisely use Grace for the benefit of others (1 Pet. 4:10). If you waste Grace, He can take it away (Matt. 25:14-30)!

What is God's Spirit Saying to Me...
As I Navigate Life According To 1 Peter

2 PETER

Turning Your Worst Nightmare... Into Your Greatest Victory!

Do you know anyone whose life has been turned into a Living Nightmare? Hellish circumstances and intimidating people can steal away the joy of living...even for strong Christians. ***But in God, there is hope!***

- What's a "Living" Nightmare and who can you go to for help?
- What was going on in Peter's world that caused him to write this letter?
- Four ways God helps you to Live Victoriously even in the midst of your worst nightmare.

Turning Your Worst Nightmare...
Into Your Greatest Victory!

What's your worst nightmare? Is it something you're dreading...or are you living in it right <u>Now</u>? Real-life nightmares usually involve loss... loss of health, loss of relationships, loss of freedom, loss of finances, loss of career, loss of family closeness or loss of a loved one. But unlike a bad dream, you can't just wake up and shake off the emotions. You have to live with your loss day after day after day. So, where can you go for help? Psychologists may help you deal with the psychological pain. Psychiatrists can prescribe emotion-deadening medication. *But only God can turn a nightmare circumstance into a victorious life.*

For Christians living in 67AD, their worst nightmare was Nero...the demonic emperor of Rome, drunk with power and insane with cruelty. In those days it was a crime to be a Christian. The penalty was imprisonment, torture and death! As the severity of persecution increased, so did the anxiety of God's people. Even Peter, the great apostle of Jesus, knew his life would end at any moment (2 Pet. 1:14-15). That's why he wrote this letter. *In the midst of their worst nightmare, he revealed how to live victoriously. Though events and people change throughout time, the pain of suffering is still the same. And so are the principles that Peter gave Christians 2,000 years ago.*

1. <u>REMIND</u> Yourself Who You Really Are (2 Pet. 1:2-4). Suffering and pain can cause even a strong believer to have "Spiritual Amnesia." That's why Peter had to remind Christians who they really were in Christ (2 Pet. 1:12-13). You are <u>NOT</u> the victim of your circumstances. Why? Because God's power makes you a partaker in His <u>LIFE</u> through Jesus. *That means you are <u>IN</u> the eternal God and the eternal God is <u>IN</u> you. You're not by yourself. God is right there with you even in life's nightmares (Ps. 139:7-12).*

2. Now That You Know Who You Really Are, Begin to <u>ACT</u> Like It (2 Pet. 1:5-11). Do your <u>best</u> to add to your faith these seven virtues: *"Good Character, Spiritual Understanding, Alert Discipline, Passionate Patience, Reverent Wonder, Warm Friendliness, and Generous Love"* (Message Bible). Don't take these lightly, my friend. ***The more you focus on these things, the less important your suffering will be. That's how your faith grows. That's how you know for certain that you will live forever with God.***

3. Don't Allow <u>DECEPTIVE TEACHING</u> To Pervert Your Faith (2 Pet. 2:1-22)! Nero wasn't the only "nightmare" that Christians had to endure. False prophets and false teachers were twisting true doctrine concerning the Savior and re-defining how people should live. They were mixing world philosophies and sensual lifestyles with Christianity and calling it "Freedom." ***Don't follow them...or else you may be lured into their destruction with them (2 Pet. 3:16-17)!***

4. Remember, <u>GOD IS BIGGER</u> Than Your Little World (2 Pet. 3:1-18). Life is short and eternity is <u>F O R E V E R</u>! Even those who live to be 100 will die and have to stand before the Lord to give an account for how they lived. Peter reminded the suffering believers that one day Jesus will return. And when He does, He will destroy all that is evil and restore the world back to righteousness. In that day, all suffering will be removed and the faithful in Christ will be glorified (Rom. 8:17-18). ***A Victorious Life is one that is lived in such a way as to spend forever in the presence of the Lord.***

So then, how can you navigate your destiny according to 2 Peter? Follow Peter's directions and you will be able to turn your nightmare into a testimony of God's grace for the world to see. Trust in God's love for you and His Spirit will deliver you from all evil...even while you're suffering. **Now that's called Victorious Living!**

What is God's Spirit Saying to Me...
As I Navigate Life According To 2 Peter

1 JOHN

The Enemy Within (Part 1)
"The Spirit of Antichrist!"

The Antichrist! Is it the very incarnation of evil? Is it an extraordinarily wicked human being? Is it a monstrous beast rising out of the sea? *Or maybe it's working in some preachers and teachers today!?*

- Who was the Antichrist of John's Day?
- Where was it working and what was it doing?
- How can you STOP this force of evil from influencing your life?

The Enemy Within (Part 1)
"The Spirit of Antichrist!"

You've got to hand it to Hollywood. They really know how to make nail-biting, hair-raising, action-packed, thriller spy movies. What's their secret? **Mystery! Suspense! Infiltration! Conspiracy! Betrayal!** Then they throw in a **Switch Ending**...the "good-guy" you trusted ends up being the BAD-GUY! He's the **"Enemy Within"** who secretly schemes to overthrow the good-guys and establish his control. Where does Hollywood come up with these plots? *It's Real Life!* And why does this happen in real life? *The world is unknowingly mimicking the greatest intrigue and betrayal of all time: Lucifer's insurrection against God (Rev. 12:7-9; Is. 14:12-15; Ezek. 28:12-17)!* **Satan's strategy for overthrowing God's work through the church hasn't changed... Infiltrate and Betray! Such was the case when John wrote this letter.**

The first century world, as one commentator wrote, was *"a babel of religious voices."* Each one was whispering (perhaps screaming) in the ears of the young church. Their intention was to either prove Christianity wrong or to *"amalgamate the Gospel with prevailing philosophies and systems of thought."* Who were those who tried to twist the truth of who Jesus was into a different Gospel (2 Cor. 11:3-4)? *John called them "Antichrists"...those who refuse to believe that Jesus is the incarnate God (1 John 4:2-3). And neither do they hold to the teachings of Jesus as revealed in Scripture (2 John 7-9).* So, what else does John teach us about the antichrist? Read this carefully and be forewarned.

1. Antichrist Is a <u>SPIRIT</u>...The Enemy of God Who Works Through People (1 John 4:1-4). Evil masterfully disguises itself as good. According to John and Peter, it masquerades as *prophets, teachers and fellow believers* (2 Pet. 2:1). Will there be one powerful world leader that arises as <u>THE</u> Antichrist? Some think so. However, this spirit works in many people to

disrupt the work of God's church (1 John 2:18). *Its agenda: Make you doubt the Absolutes of the Christian Faith!*

2. He's a Con-Man Who Loves to Work <u>INSIDE</u> the Church (1 John 2:18-19). According to this passage, those who John calls "antichrists" were once INSIDERS! John agreed with Paul concerning these evil people who <u>infiltrate</u> the lives of believers to deceive them (2 Tim. 3:1-9). Paul says it's the "man of lawlessness" who sits in the very house of God (2 Thess. 2:3-4)! *Again, his agenda is <u>Apostasy</u>...he causes believers to Fall Away from the truth of who Jesus really is!*

3. He Offers an <u>ALTERNATIVE</u> to the "Whole Counsel" of God's Word (Acts 20:27-30). Deceptive spirits love to wrench God's word out of its proper context. They take away the need for repentance and personal faith in Jesus as a requirement for salvation (1 John 4:2-6). They're experts at preaching one portion of scripture that agrees with their heretical concepts while leaving out the whole counsel of God that refutes their claims. *That, my friend, is not just doctrinal error...it's a demonic undermining of the very foundation of the Christian Faith!*

4. So, What Can You Do to <u>STOP</u> Him In His Tracks? Actually, it's embarrassingly simple. <u>Just Read Your Bible and Believe It!</u> That's why most of John's letter instructed believers about the True Doctrines of our Faith: Salvation is a personal Relationship with Jesus. But you can't continually live in sin and still think you have salvation (1 John 1:5 - 2:6). People who do not believe (have faith) in Jesus as God in the Flesh, are NOT saved (1 John 2:22-23; 4:2-3)! *The best defense against the Spirit of Antichrist is a rock-solid personal understanding of Biblical Truth concerning Jesus and Salvation! Without it you're Antichrist bait!*

Hey folks...I'm not making this stuff up! This really *IS* what John wrote about! Just read it for yourself! And guess what? The Spirit of Antichrist is still at work today! **Don't miss the next teaching: Part 2 of The Enemy Within - "Gullible Christians!"**

What is God's Spirit Saying to Me...
As I Navigate Life According To 1 John

2 JOHN

The Enemy Within (Part 2)
"Gullible Christians!"

What's worse than the Spirit of Antichrist? Gullible people who give him a hide-out in God's Church! Inconceivably, it happened in the early church. *And tragically it's happening in today's churches as well!*

- Why did John write this second letter and what was going on?
- What makes people so gullible?
- How can you protect yourself against the workings of the Spirit of the Antichrist?

The Enemy Within (Part 2)
"Gullible Christians!"

"If you're too open-minded, your brains will fall out!"..."Artificial intelligence is no match for natural stupidity."..."Someone who thinks logically provides a nice contrast to the real world." We love to make jokes about people who get fooled. But if we're the ones who have been deceived, it's no laughing matter! Gullibility ruins lives, destroys self-confidence and leaves you broke, angry and feeling like a fool! Yet Christians who love the Lord with all their hearts are not immune to being duped by shrewd deceivers. Case in point: ***Christians in the early church!*** That's why John wrote this personal letter to the churches. It was a warning to his friends to avoid these dangers.

What a horrifying thought...that Christians would naively open their doors to the antichrist himself! But that's exactly what John said would happen if the early church didn't carefully discern those who came among them. Some with itching-ears for "new truth" were actually inviting antichrists (those opposing the teachings of Christ) into their homes (2 John 7-11; 2 Tim. 3:6-9). But their "truth" was laced with spiritual poison! Soon it sickened minds and led the gullible into false doctrines that destroyed their faith. John was so appalled at their foolishness that he commanded, *"Do not receive them into your house and do not give them a greeting! For the one who gives them a greeting participates in their evil deeds!" (2 John 10-11).* ***The "Enemy Within" wasn't only the spirit of antichrist...it was also Gullible Christians who entertained their false doctrines!*** So, what makes people so gullible? Consider this:

1. **Some People May Just Be Born That Way.** Some scientists believe that naivety is an unfortunate part of a person's DNA. Whether it's true or not, you don't have to stay that way! *If you get duped once, you're a victim. If you get fooled repeatedly, you're a volunteer (Prov. 14:15)!*

2. **Some Are Magnets for Stupidity!** Nearly 2,100 years ago Plato taught, "Whatever deceives men seems to produce a magical enchantment." *That, my friend, is the "Fallen Nature." Like a moth to a flame, people who flirt with deceptive doctrines are consumed by them (Prov. 14:18)!*

3. **Others "Want What They Want" Too Much!** People would rather find what they HOPE for than to discover TRUTH. *It may be a lucrative investment, a "perfect" mate or a doctrine that promises heaven without faith in Jesus. Remember, without due diligence you'll get bamboozled!*

What can you do about it? How can you protect yourself against deceptive belief systems?

1. **Remember, You're Dealing with Highly Skilled Manipulators!** They know all the right words to say. They're experts on half-truths. They know exactly how to endear themselves to you and make you trust them. *Learn to identify their flattery and you'll escape their snare (Prov. 29:5)!*

2. **Develop a "Sanctified" Skepticism!** Don't be too trusting. In other words...use your logic, reasoning and common sense. As John wrote, put doctrines to the test (1 John 4:1). *Examine your own Bible to see whether the things you're hearing are true or not (Acts 17:11).*

3. **Learn How To "Connect The Dots!"** Don't ignore the little indicators that point to inconsistencies. If a spiritual leader's private words don't line up with their public persona...Watch Out! If you receive too many public compliments from the pulpit, you're being set up! *If what you're hearing doesn't agree with scripture...RUN! (Prov. 27:12).*

4. **Fill Your Heart with the Genuine...and the Counterfeit Will Never Find a Place in Your Life!** As one writer put it, when genuine faith is questioned, it creates a vacuum ready to suck in some new form of belief. *Gullible Christians are "vacuum cleaners" filled with the world's garbage!*

Don't miss the next teaching: Part 3 of The Enemy Within - "Control Freaks!"

What is God's Spirit Saying to Me...
As I Navigate Life According To 2 John

3 JOHN

The Enemy Within (Part 3)
"Control Freaks!"

As much as we would like to think that the early church was an ideal community of Christian love and conduct...it wasn't! *There were contentions, arrogance and abrasive people...just like today!*

- What was going on in the early church that pressed John to write this letter?
- What are Control Freaks and what causes people to become them?
- Are there any Biblical solutions for dealing with controlling people in the church?

The Enemy Within (Part 3)
"Control Freaks!"

Diotrephes was a control freak! Some Bible commentators believe this man, who John named in his third letter, may have been an <u>early monarchial bishop</u> or a <u>church leader</u> who abused his position of authority. Others thought him to be an <u>ambitious layperson</u> that exerted his dominant personality to control others. But all agree on this: Diotrephes was a contentious, proud, arrogant and self-centered individual who refused all authority except his own! *He even took it upon himself to kick Christians out of his church who didn't agree with him (3 John 9-10)!* Consequently, John, the "Apostle of Love," had to deal harshly with Diotrephes. Why? *Because he was a divisive enemy of God's cause working from within the church itself!*

Control freaks! You know who they are. *They're the alpha-male (or female), micromanager, take-charge, my-way-or-the-highway kind of people.* They're your supervisors, your co-workers, your friends and even your family members. In fact, you may be living with one right now! And heaven forbid...<u>YOU</u> may have some of these tendencies yourself! *Unfortunately, these abrasive people even show up in the church of the Living God!* So what causes people to develop "Control-Freak" actions? Are there any antidotes to this intimidating psychological behavior? Here's what I've discovered:

1. **A "Control" Freak Is, Well, "Out-of-Control!"** God, by virtue of His eternal nature and sovereign authority, rules the world in righteousness, justice and truth (Ps. 89:14). Created in His image, God gave people the power to rule with Him. But sin distorts God's intentions. Instead of taking charge of their own lives and representing God's righteousness, the fallen nature in controlling people abuses others to advance their own cause. *Like Diotrephes, Control Freaks remove God's holy*

governance and operate outside of His righteous purposes. That's called, "Out-of-Control!"

2. **They're Ambitious Power-Seekers.** The Eerdmans Bible dictionary describes Diotrephes like this: *"Eager to help fill the vacuum in leadership being created as more and more apostles were approaching old age and dying, Diotrephes objected to John's lingering ecclesiastical authority."* *If you can't wait for the "old man" to retire or die, you're on the thin ice of being a Control Freak!*

3. **Control Freaks Are Actually Driven by Insecurity and Fear!** Most psychologists agree with this conclusion. The more secure an individual is, the less he or she feels the need to control others! *If you're afraid you'll lose your place of authority, you'll adopt Control Freak behavior. If you're threatened by people's freedom of choice, you'll try to take it away from them!*

4. **However, True Leaders Are Never Control Freaks!** Real leaders lead by vision, direction and inspiration. They draw followers by their proven character and God-given abilities. They never Control people...they **Serve** them (Matt. 20:20-28), **Stir** them to action and **Release** their potential for greatness. *If you rule by fear and intimidation, you're not a leader at all...you're a Dictator!*

What's The Solution to Control Freaks in the Church? *True Apostolic Authority!* The Apostle Paul set the record straight in Eph. 4:11-16 concerning the purpose of leadership in God's Church. *They are to "Equip" (literally: "Restore") people to the full image of who God intends them to be in Christ and to Protect them from deception.* In the case of Diotrephes, who ruled with an iron hand, it meant that John had to deal swiftly against his perverted base of authority (3 John 10). *God's true leaders Commend those who lead properly (3 John 1-4, 11-12) and they Teach the characteristics of a righteous leader (1*

Tim. 3:1-13; Titus 1:7-11). If you believe you are called to be a leader in God's church, take heed to the warnings in this short letter of the Apostle John. Follow the "Map" of God's word and His Spirit will lead you to greatness.

What is God's Spirit Saying to Me...
As I Navigate Life According To 3 John

JUDE

This Is a Real Game-Changer
It'll Cause You to "Grow Up" in a Hurry!

Growing to maturity is the goal of all Christians. But it's painful when you realize that some people who call themselves "Christians," aren't. *Jude's short letter is quite a shocker...but it'll shock you into maturity!*

- What was Jude's Game-Changing message?
- Who were the predators he was writing about?
- What can you do to protect yourself against them today?

This Is a Real Game-Changer
It'll Cause You to "Grow Up" in a Hurry!

It was a Game-Changing Moment for Jude. Repeatedly he sat down to write a "nice" letter about the wondrous salvation that Christians shared in common. But he couldn't do it. *Deep within his spirit he was so disturbed by what he saw in the Christian community that he abandoned his original thoughts and penned this solemn warning instead.* Compelled by God's Spirit, Jude wrote of an angelic battle that came to the earth (Jude 6; Rev. 12:7-9). Evil had entered flesh and drew people into a web of deception and defilement (Jude 4, 7-8). Jude saw good-hearted believers with Passive faith being swept away by evil men. His letter exposed their demonic strategy and fervently admonished his readers to *"Contend"* (fight intensely) for what they believed (Jude 3). What was happening? *False teachers were spreading faith-destroying heresies that corrupted naïve souls (Jude 4)!*

A Game-Changer is a complete change in the way something is done or thought about. It's a new strategy that, when fully executed, will alter the overall outcome of an athletic event, a business venture, or a person's life. In other words, it determines what happens to your Destiny! It's interesting that Jude chose the word *"Contend"* when exhorting his fellow believers. *This Greek word speaks of a "place of contest, an arena or stadium" where athletic games were held or gladiators fought for their lives!* Take a few minutes to read again Jude's short letter. It will open your eyes to the conflict around you. It will warn you of predators that seek to destroy your soul! It will awaken you from a lethargic belief system to a battle-ready faith. *Jude's letter was indeed a Game-Changer...it caused believers to "Grow Up" in a hurry!* Listen to his warnings:

1. You Can't Trust Everybody In Your Church (Jude 4)! *Wow, that's a Game-Changer!* Even the early church had false teachers among them. If someone (regardless of who they are

or the position they hold) tells you that God's grace will allow you to ignore moral attitudes and behaviors found in scripture, it's a lie! *If your Bible doesn't allow it, neither should you (Jude 7)!*

2. **Don't Accept "Revelatory" Truth Based on Sources Other Than the Christian Bible (Jude 8).** False shepherds in the early church claimed they had "special" knowledge that came through dreams and world philosophies. They rejected apostolic authority and mocked redemptive truth they didn't understand (Jude 10-13). *If you follow them, you'll end up like them...Doubly Dead!*

3. **Don't Fall for the Oldest Tricks in the Book...Disguise and Flattery!** These false leaders would partake in Christian celebrations under the pretense of being a believer. But, they were like hidden reefs that sink ships (Jude 12, NASB). They use flattery (sometimes publicly) to endear hearts to believe their lies (Jude 16). *Even Paul warned about these false apostles in 2 Cor. 11:13-15.*

Jude's letter can be a **Game-Changer** for you as well...if you want to "Grow Up" in Christ. This is the assignment of true Apostles, Prophets, Evangelists, Pastors and Teachers (Eph. 4:11-16)! Don't take this lightly, my friend. *This is a Present Day Crisis, and your Eternal Destiny is determined by your decisions.*

1. **Don't Ignore the Warnings Written by the Apostles of Jesus (Jude 17-19).** Jesus warned us that this would happen (Matt. 7:15-23). So did His apostles (Acts 20:29-30; 1 Tim. 4:1-2; 2 Pet. 2:1).

2. **Build Yourself Up in the "Most Holy" Faith (Jude 20-21).** This is not a "mixture" of beliefs; it's a pure and personal belief in Jesus as the ONLY way to receive eternal life. When you read

your Bible and pray regularly it's like exercise...it strengthens you for the battle.

3. **Become a "Rescuer" of Others (Jude 22-25).** Many a poor soul has been led astray into deception. Learn how to *"Snatch them out of the fire!"* Christianity is not a passive belief system...it's a BATTLE for the souls of men. *Those who lose this battle...lose their souls forever (Matt. 16:25-26)! But those who trust in Jesus will never stumble!*

What is God's Spirit Saying to Me...
As I Navigate Life According To Jude

REVELATION

The Great "Mystery" of God Is Finished! But What Happens Next?

Well, this is it...the LAST book of the Bible. Many misunderstand it and some use it to try to scare people into heaven. *But few realize that it's God's answers to all human questions about life. Don't miss this!*

- What's going to happen AFTER the world ends?
- What does the Bible mean when it says the "Mystery" of God?
- Five questions about Life and its struggles that God answers in the book of Revelation.

The Great "Mystery" of God Is Finished! But What Happens Next?

The book of Revelation can be very confusing. Scholars agree that it describes the "End of the World." *But what happens **AFTER** the world ends?* At the end of this book, everything turns out okay...but NOT for everyone! If the Lord Jesus is your Savior, you'll enjoy these insights that many Christians never think about.

John began this final book of the Bible with these words, "The ***Revelation*** of Jesus Christ." The term "Revelation" comes from the Greek, *"apokalupsis"*...or "Apocalypse," which means to separate the veil, to disclose long hidden secrets, to uncover a mystery. When the Bible uses the word "Mystery," it's not like a Hollywood movie. *It's "God's secret counsels which govern His redemptive purposes. These are hidden from ungodly and wicked men but are made plain to the godly."* In other words, God shares His eternal plan with YOU...but NOT with unbelievers. *It's a "Mystery" they just can't figure out!*

Have you ever asked God "WHY?" *Why* was I born? *Why* is there evil in the world with so much suffering and injustice? *Why* did Jesus build His Church and then let internal scandal destroy people's faith? *Why* doesn't God stop these things from happening? *Why* do I have to grow old and die? Finally, *What's* the point of all this? Well guess what? *When the End of the World comes, the next thing that happens is "**REVELATION!**"* When *"The Mystery of God is Finished"* (Rev. 10:7), the veil will be pulled back, the pieces of life's puzzle will come together and it will all make sense. *Though it's not possible to fully understand it now, God reveals a glimpse of His purposes in this amazing book.*

1. <u>WHY</u> Was I Born? This mystery is answered in **Rev. 1:5-6**. You were born to be Royalty...sons and daughters of the Eternal King, God Himself! You were created to represent

God's righteous rule on the earth as His "kingdom" and His "priests." *Though sin disqualified you from His purposes, redemption through the blood of His Son restores believers to their royal Destiny.*

2. <u>WHY</u> Is There Evil in the World with so Much Suffering and Injustice in Life? This intriguing mystery is revealed in **Rev. 12:1-17.** God did not create evil...it occurred when Lucifer (Satan) and his angels chose to rebel against God and were cast to the earth. Gullible people bought into his lies and followed his pattern of evil. But God sent His Son to destroy the works of the devil and to deliver all who trust in His Son. *Now <u>YOU</u> have God's power to overcome Satan in your own life.*

3. <u>WHY</u> Did Jesus Build His Church, Then Let Internal Scandal Destroy People's Faith? **Rev. 2-3** explains this mystery in the corrections that Jesus gave to His Church. His Church is His redeemed people whom He charges to guard the Faith (Matt. 7:15-23; Acts 20:28-32). *God doesn't just "Let" scandal come into His Church...He gives <u>YOU</u> authority to deal with it!*

4. <u>WHY</u> Doesn't God Stop These Things From Happening? The answer to that mystery is **Rev. 2:21-23**...*Freedom of Will!* God granted to angels and all people the ability to choose right from wrong...along with rewards or consequences that follow. *Yet, in His grace, God warns us when we stray off course and He gives us <u>Time to Repent</u> (2 Pet. 3:9; Jer. 18:7-11). But for those who don't, the consequences are Eternal!*

5. <u>WHY</u> Do I Have to Grow Old and Die? <u>WHAT'S</u> the Point of All This? The aging process and ultimate death wasn't God's idea. God warned Adam that sin would bring death, but he would not listen...and neither do we! *But, for those who love God and His Son, He demonstrates His Mercy, Grace and Power by REVERSING evil and giving us Life Eternal!* This final Mystery is revealed in **Rev. 11:15; 21:3-12 and 22:3.**

When this great "Mystery of God is Finished," we will join with all the redeemed in declaring, *"Who will not fear You, O Lord, and bring glory to Your name? For You alone are holy. All nations will come and worship before You, for Your righteous acts HAVE BEEN REVEALED." (Rev. 15:4)*

What is God's Spirit Saying to Me...
As I Navigate Life According To Revelation

EPILOGUE

What Then Shall I Do?

Inspiration without the Practical "How-To's" can be frustrating. It's like revving up your motor without knowing how to drive or where to go. If the Bible is God's "Map" and His Spirit is His "Compass," then it's essential to learn how to use these Divine Navigational Gifts.

- How can I study God's Word so that it becomes my "Map"?
- How does God's Spirit become His "Compass" for my life?
- How do these work together to help me reach my Destiny in Christ?

How Can I Study "The Map" of God's Word?

If you're planning a trip across the United States, you'll need to purchase road maps to know which towns you'll pass through, where you can eat, spend the night and see the sights. And, of course, you must know the highways to take to arrive at your destination.

Likewise, the Map of God's Word is a record of men and women who successfully navigated life and arrived at their Destinations in God. It also tells the tragic stories of those who failed and lost their way. Without God's Map, you'll become lost...physically, emotionally and spiritually. Here's how you should begin your life-journey with God:

1. **Begin Building Your Personal Bible Reference Library.**
   Bible References are guides that help you understand what the Bible is saying, what certain words mean and how you can look up key information. The basic Bible References include:

   - **A "Study Bible."** This is a Bible with helpful information about each book of the Bible. It also includes Bible Verse Cross References. They point to similar passages that give added dimensions of understanding. When selecting a Study Bible, choose a version that's easy for you to read and understand.

   - **A Bible Commentary.** Commentaries give a verse by verse explanation of what each passage in the Bible means.

   - **A Bible Dictionary.** It's important to know what words in the Bible mean and who important people are in the Bible.

   - **An English Dictionary.** Don't forget this resource. It gives added depth to the meanings of English words you read.

   - **A Concordance.** This is a handy tool to help you look up and find where certain words in the Bible are located.

2. Set Aside Study Time Each Week.
   You can do this a little each day, or schedule an entire morning or evening...whatever works best for you. The main idea is consistency. Blend reading with study so that you know what you're reading. If you read a word or a passage you don't understand...look it up in your Commentary and Dictionaries. You'll be surprised at how much insight you'll gain!

3. Understand the Big Picture...God's Overall Intention.
   The Word of God is all about **Restoration**. It's how God redeems and restores fallen people and a corrupt world back to Himself (John 20:31; Luke 19:10; Acts 3:18-20). It helps people to discover their **Identities** and how to fulfill God's **Assignment** for them on the earth (2 Tim. 3:15-17).

4. Develop an Orderly Way of Thinking...Ask Key Questions and Pay Attention to Details.

   - Let's say you're interested in a specific topic...like raising children, a personal issue you're struggling with, or an area that involves a major decision you're facing.

     1) Look up key words about the topic in your Bible Concordance; 2) Write down the scriptures that you believe would shed some light on the issue; 3) Find and read those scriptures in your Bible. For proper context, be sure to read the passages above and below the one you've found.

   - Use Your "Study Bible" to Discover What a Scripture Means in its Proper Context.

     Who was the author and why was this particular book written? What was happening in the life of the author? What is the chapter or paragraph emphasizing? Who's talking to who and why? What was the "present crisis" when this passage was written and who were the people it was addressed to? **Without proper context, you can easily misinterpret and misapply God's Word!**

- **What Does the Rest of Scripture and Bible Scholars Say About This Passage?**
  Look up the cross references in the side margins of your Bible. Follow the trails through Scripture and let Scripture explain itself. Don't exclude passages that you may not understand or agree with. Read what proven Christian scholars (past and present) have written about the passage.

5. **Discover Spiritual Principles that Transcend Time and Culture.**
   Spiritual Principles are Spiritual Laws (like sowing and reaping), God's Character and His Purposes, Patterns of God's Ways for us to follow, Patterns of man's Failures for us to avoid, and Promises from God that can be received only through obedience and covenant with Him.

6. **Application, Application, Application!** *(Me First, then Others— 1 Cor. 9:27)*
   How does this passage address my needs and inspire me toward my potential? How does this help me to negotiate the storms in my life and give me solutions and hope for my circumstances? How does this motivate me to grow in faith, serve God and reach my Destiny in Christ?

7. **Finally, Plan Ahead! Look at Your Map BEFORE You Make Major Decisions.**
   Life is made up of the decisions and choices we make. They determine the road we take, the quality of our lives and the final destination where we end up. If you violate the Principles found in God's word, you'll end up lost and destroyed! Why? Because God knows what's BEST for us and He warns us when we begin to get off course (Is. 48:17-19 NIV). The more familiar you are with the Map of God's Word, the less likely you are to end up at the wrong destination in life.

How Do I Follow the "Compass" of God's Spirit?

The Holy Spirit is like a Divine Compass...it always points to Truth. Remember, TRUTH is not a concept or philosophy of life. It's a Person...the Second Person of the Triune God! Jesus is the Way, the **Truth** and the Life. It's impossible to get to the Father, except through Him (John 14:6). Since Jesus is the "Living" Word (John 1:1), the "Written" Word (the Scriptures) bear witness to who Jesus really is (John 5:39). He's God's Son sent to redeem fallen humanity back to God the Father. Therefore, God the Spirit (the Holy Spirit) is the Spirit of Truth (John 15:26) who always points to Jesus in your Bible. *So, what must you do if you are to be led by God's Compass?*

1. First and Foremost, Get the "Compass" in Your Heart.
   When you receive Jesus as your Lord and Savior, He sends His Spirit (the Holy Spirit) to reside in your heart...sort of like an "on-board" Compass (Gal. 4:4-6). From that vantage point, He is able to guide your heart into truth and reveal the wisdom of Jesus to you (John 16:13-15). *Remember, your heart is the center of your desires and emotions. That's why He lives there...because your heart is the rudder of your life!*

2. Cooperate With His Sanctifying Work In Your Life.
   Sanctification is the on-going process of being healed (purified) from your former life before Christ became your Savior (1 Pet. 1:2). The Holy Spirit is the One who renews your mind and helps you to "put on" the New Self which is created in righteousness (Eph. 4:22-29). *One of His assignments is to prepare you to be the Bride of Christ (Rev. 19:7; 21:2).*

3. Be Sensitive to the Leading (Direction) of the Holy Spirit.
   At times God's Spirit will disagree with YOUR plans. He can close a door that you want to walk through and then open another door that leads to a different opportunity (Acts 16:6-10). Why? Perhaps there could be danger or entrapment in

the way you wanted to go. Or maybe God just simply knows what's best for you. Possibly He has a greater work for you to do elsewhere. *And don't put a time-limit on God's work in your life. The fulfillment of your ministry may be weeks, months or years away. Just know that God's "Compass" will never lead you astray.*

4. Open Your Heart to Receive Spiritual Gifts From the Lord.
As a Christian, you are part of the Family of God who loves, encourages and cares for one another. For this reason God's Spirit desires to give you spiritual gifts so you can minister to your brothers and sisters in Christ and "build them up" in the faith. Read Rom. 12:4-8; Eph. 4:11-16 and 1 Cor. 12–14 to see what these gifts are and how God wants you to use them. *This is God's "Compass" working at its best. He points you in the right direction and empowers you to help others. Then you become a witness to the world of the grace and love of God.*

5. Always Remain Tenderhearted Before God.
Believe it or not, God's Spirit is actually very sensitive and can be easily grieved (Eph. 4:30). Like a parent who intensely grieves over the rebellion of a wayward child, so it is with God. God's Spirit, who lives within you, "feels" distress and sorrow when your actions betray His righteous intentions for your life. But when a child has a tender heart toward his parent, he will quickly repent for fear of <u>disappointing</u> his mother or father whom he loves. *Tenderhearted means that you're quick to repent when you sense the Spirit's grief over your actions.* It's not the fear of God's punishment that makes you want to repent, it's godly sorrow knowing that your actions fall short of the person who God has created you to be. *You are His child, redeemed from the gutters of life to live righteously with Him...forever!*

How Does the Map and Compass Work Together To Help Me Reach My Destiny in Christ?

In centuries past, before there were highways and directional signs, travelers depended upon maps and compasses to navigate their way through forests, over mountains and along rivers to arrive at their destinations. With maps they could chart their courses and with compasses they would be certain that they stayed on course. God's Word is the Map that allows you to chart your course for your Destiny in Christ. God's Spirit keeps you on course for that Destiny. *This means you must take the time to READ the Bible*...or else you won't know how to chart your course. Then, when you do, *the Holy Spirit brings to your remembrance* the things you've read...especially during critical junctures and dramas in your life (John 14:26). Here's how they work together:

1. Let's say you're a young man or woman desiring marriage. How can you determine if you've found the right person?
   Because you've read God's Word, the Holy Spirit can remind you of the following scriptural principles:
   - Ps. 23. Ladies, if a future husband isn't a "shepherd" that cares for your soul, you're in for a disappointment.
   - Prov. 31:10-31. Men, look for these character traits and you will have found a treasure.
   - Eph. 5:21-31. Men, this is God's pattern for you to follow.

2. If you're looking for a fulfilling career, where do you start?
   Because you've read the Bible, the Holy Spirit will remind you of these Biblical principles:
   - Prov. 16:3 & 9. Commit to the Lord the kind of work that you desire for a career and then God will direct your steps.
   - Luke 16:12. Be faithful to work as a "trainee" in the career of your choice and you will be trusted with more.

3. What if you receive a disturbing doctor's report?
   God is gracious and kind. His desire is for you to fulfill your Destiny in Him...even in the face of health problems. God's "Compass" will lead you to Biblical principles such as these:
   - **James 5:14-16.** God honors the prayers of the elders of your church. Trust the Lord to heal you and raise you up.
   - **Matt. 8:14-15.** When God raises you up, use your healing as an extension on your life to serve and help others.

4. If your teenage children are straying from the way you raised them, what can you do?
   God's "Map" tells you how to handle this. His "Compass" brings back to your remembrance these passages:
   - **Prov. 22:6.** Pray and trust God to bring your children back to the foundation of righteousness that you built in them.
   - **Luke 15:11-32.** Don't give up hope. Trust that God will bring them back to his senses. Then welcome them home.

5. What should you do when you are betrayed by someone so close to you that it threatens to destroy your life?
   - **John 13:1-15.** Remember, Jesus washed the feet of Judas, the very one who was betraying Him.
   - **Luke 23:34.** Forgiveness is Redemptive...it gives your betrayer an example of what God did for you.

6. As you grow into your "Senior" years, how should you handle the changes that take place in your body and life?
   - **Is. 46:4.** Continue to trust the Lord in your old age as you did when you were young. God will take care of you!
   - **Ps. 71:17-18.** Continue to declare God's wonders to your generation and impart His wisdom and counsel to the next.

Other Books Written By Dan Rhodes

My prayer is that this book has been a blessing to you and that you've been able to glean wisdom and truth from God's Word for your life. May the Lord continue to richly bless you and lead you in His everlasting way...now and forevermore.

I invite you to visit our Destiny Navigators website to review some of the other books and postings that are made available to you and your loved ones. *www.DestinyNavigators.org*

"Setting Your Heart on the Kingdom"

A 12-Book Series - Daily Devotional Teachings from every book of the Bible. Principles of the Kingdom of God are surfaced with practical applications for life

"Becoming a Seeker of God's Kingdom"

A Workbook Study Guide - A "fill-in-the-blank" Teaching Manual on the Kingdom with Life-Application Assignments. Available in Teacher and Student Editions.

"Discovering Your Destiny"

A Workbook Study Guide Series - Your final destination isn't a distant island or land...it's living in God's gracious plan that enhances your true identity.

"Once Upon A Kingdom"

Available Soon - The Epic Story of Good and Evil, Human Destiny and God's Eternal Purposes written on the backdrop of medieval days of Kings, Kingdoms, Knights and Dragons.

Made in the USA
Charleston, SC
21 September 2015